BOROUGH OF TWICKENHAM
LOCAL HISTORY SOC

Paper N

KNELLER HALL

LOOKING BACKWARD LOOKING FORWARD

ED HARRIS

ISBN: 978-1-911145-03-5 Price £6.00

Contents

Cover picture: Rear of the house and grounds from Humphry Repton's *Red Book for Whitton Hall* 1796.

INTRODUCTION

THE PUBLIC ANNOUNCEMENT made in January 2016 by the Ministry of Defence (MOD) of its intention to close the Royal Military School of Music at Kneller Hall was met with a statement from the Leader of Richmond-upon-Thames council (where the school sits) declaring 'we need to make sure that the history of the site and its open space is protected.' While all of the likely physical manifestations of the eventual outcome will be subject to planning requirements, its complete history has never been written. That is the purpose of this publication.

The two books written about Kneller Hall focus primarily on the development of military music in the British army. The first, *A Hundred Years of Military Music* was published in 1959 and offers a precursor to the pre-history of the estate that has become the repository of highly skilled musicians. *The Trumpets Will Sound*, published in 1996 sets out a more substantial historical scene in its celebration of the Royal Military School of Music that has succeeded in creating a new level of professionalism making British bands the standard for military music worldwide across a century and more.

This publication widens the history of what is the last remaining landed estate in Whitton, Middlesex; a circumstance amply identified in the House of Commons by Tania Mathias, MP for Twickenham, in 2016.[1] Responding to the proposed sale of Kneller Hall she declared it to be 'more than that. It is about Whitton, and Whitton's history.' Within the context of about a dozen Ministry of Defence sites for sale, 'Kneller Hall is the exceptional one in that list,' she maintained, 'because this is not about a building, but about a community. It is no ordinary building and no ordinary site. Kneller Hall in effect is Whitton, and Whitton is Kneller Hall.'

Mark Lancaster, the Parliamentary Under-Secretary of State for Defence replied by thanking his Right Honourable Friend for the commendable support she expressed for her community and assured her that the concerns and feelings of the local community were always paramount as part the decision-making process. However, as part of the Government's 'Prosperity Agenda,' the MOD was committed to releasing land to contribute towards 55,000 new housing units called for by Parliament. These plans were not directed at individual communities, regiments or bases, he affirmed, but having Government funding in the right place to ensure the continued defence and security of the entire United Kingdom.

This is a local history paper and by definition parochial in its remit. But it's one with a twist. Instead of looking back entirely on events that have shaped the past, we are able to track history in the making and even help determine the future. Hence the subtitle, *Looking Backward Looking Forward*, the motto of the former Twickenham Borough Council that was in 1965 incorporated into the Greater London Borough of Richmond-upon-Thames and where Whitton now sits as an historically imprecise hinterland. A hamlet of Twickenham since Saxon times, Whitton is not a place of destination aside from the many thousands of supporters each year who pass through its railway station en route to the home of England Rugby. Less so the depleted summer concert days at Kneller Hall where a decade ago much of its open

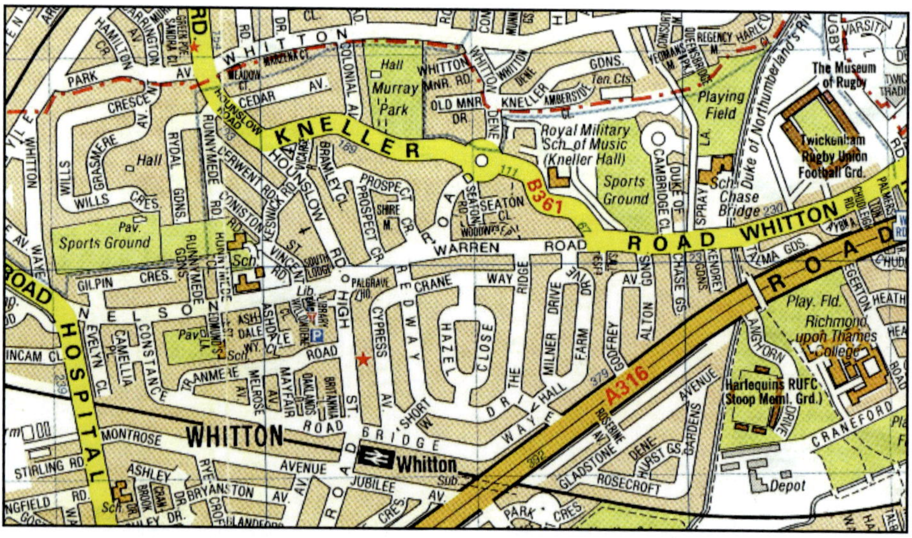

Whitton 2018. The Royal Military School of Music, Kneller Hall, is located due west of Twickenham Rugby Union Football ground (top right corner).

ground would be crammed full of cars and coaches bringing visiting promenaders to join the ranks of enthusiastic locals collectively numbering around 25,000 a year.

Education has ensured the survival of the Kneller Hall estate for over 165 years and could help determine its next incarnation should there be one. General H.R.H. The Duke of Cambridge was Commander-in-Chief of the British Army in the 1850s and is celebrated as the founder of the Military School of Music. However, his choice of Kneller Hall as its location came about quite by chance. In 1856, the Duke's focus was on providing accommodation for the London-based Guards Division. Under consideration was the Royal Military Asylum for Children of Soldiers in the Regular Army (RMA) Chelsea. Founded in 1801 by Frederick, Duke of York, the RMA was funded by the Army as home to children of fallen rank and file soldiers, at its height accommodating 1,000 boys and 500 girls.

Tasked by Cambridge to re-locate the Asylum, the RMA's Medical Officer came across a former training establishment set in countryside 10 miles west of London called Kneller Hall. When asked for an assurance that the surrounding district was a healthy place to relocate children, the Statistical Superintendent of the Registrar General's Department reported that in his opinion it was not, despite the sparsity of the population numbering a few hundred. There the mortality rate was 21 in every 1000 annually, compared to 17 in every 1000 in other parts of Middlesex, Surrey and Sussex.[2] When the Surgeon General visited Kneller Hall and carefully examined the grounds, his attention was drawn to the ancient brook that served as the boundary for the parishes of Twickenham and Isleworth. He found that even after three weeks of continuous dry weather there was insufficient drainage to obviate the likelihood of disease. To this, HRH The Duke of Cambridge requested the Commander Royal Engineers (CRE), London District, to ascertain the nature of the soil.

The CRE report was at the same time as contrary to the Surgeon General's findings as it was suggestive of a social divide where the poorer classes living about the lower levels of the hamlet were indeed more predisposed to ill-health. Deep into the 20th century many a report by the local Medical Health

Officer cited the lower levels prone to flooding, creating conditions unfit for human habitation. 'Considerable slop refuse and stable manure' was discharged into the brook that contaminated Kneller Hall's 500-yard long ornamental lake.[3] Despite this inconvenience, the CRE report declared the mansion itself to be 'well situated for a Military Asylum, its elevation commanding a good view of the surrounding countryside and enjoying a high reputation for salubrity.'[4]

As the only other means of liquid waste disposal beyond the villagers' own cesspits, fouled water passing through the estate eventually drained east into the Duke of Northumberland's River, an artificial waterway created by the Earl of Northumberland following the dissolution of the monasteries by Henry VIII in 1536. This canal effectively slashed Whitton Lands[5] in two leaving the 100-acre estate that would one day bear the name Kneller as the eastern boundary of the diminished Twickenham endship where this account is set.

1632 – 1664

MR COOKE'S HOUSE

The Domesday Book has Twickenham and Whitton incorporated into the Hounslow Hundred,[6] so we have no way of determining precisely the nature of either settlement at the time of the Norman Conquest. Hounslow Hundred was held by Walter de St-Valery, a kinsman of William who had arrived with him from Normandy. At the time of Henry VIII's dissolution of the monasteries (1536 – 1541) Sir William Chase, Sergeant at Arms to the King, held a large house, six other dwellings, five cottages and 218 acres of land in Whitton. The Lord of the Manor in 1635 was the Earl of Northumberland who commissioned cartographer Moses Glover to draw up a survey of what had become known as the Isleworth Hundred. Glover's map remains the best pictorial description of the local landscape at that time and its ongoing development, including the brook defining Twickenham parish's northern boundary, a parish that covered 1851 acres, including the hamlets of Whitton and Hethrowe (now Heathfield). Sir Simon Harvey, who organised royal journeys for Charles I, owned a large house in Whitton Dean as well as other properties and land in Whitton including a 22-acre rabbit warren and several cottages occupying the higher reaches straddling Whitton's wayward medieval road system.

In 1632 Harvey sold two of these cottages to Edmund Cooke, a Gentleman born around 1585 and who was elected a member of the parish vestry in 1622. He demolished the cottages to build the first of three substantial dwellings on the same site, the last of which comes down to us today as Kneller Hall. Clearly wealthy, Cooke's house was a statement alongside that of his immediate neighbour of rank, Sir John Suckling who built a large house in Whitton around 1604 when he was Secretary to the Lord High Treasurer. Having acquired great wealth and many properties throughout the country, Suckling improved his property at Whitton, enlarging it to incorporate a banqueting hall. He died in 1627, leaving it and £30,000 to his son, also called John, the extravagant cavalier poet. The attraction of the hamlet is clear.

Moses Glover's 1635 survey does not conform to the north south cartographic protocol we have come to accept. Hence, the site of the Rugby Football Union's ground sits to the far left of Chase Bridge (top centre) within the junction of today's Whitton Road and London Road. 'Mr. Cooke's' house is to the right of Chase Bridge just about discernable below 'WHITTNE' inscribed next to Sir John Suckling's house in the top right quarter. Cooke's house faces Peacock's farm and a row of other dwellings that would give way to the mansion of Baron John Belasyse (sometimes Ballassis) of Worlaby, who had been occupying the Suckling estate from 1671.

Death from disease in the 17th century was higher in more densely populated urban areas. The riverside centres of Twickenham and Isleworth contained larger concentrations of people more likely to contract and spread diseases such as typhus, smallpox, and tuberculosis.

Twickenham parish was then divided into four distinct quarters comprising Whitton, The Heath, Heath Lane and The Towne. Whitton, the smallest district, emerges as the most prosperous with Cooke's mansion the largest house in the parish at 20 hearths. The former Suckling mansion is the second largest at 19 hearths, and of the other 25 properties assessed, three have six hearths; four have five and four have four. After 1671, Sir Joseph Ashe's Cambridge Park in Twickenham Town tops the list at 25 hearths, followed by Lady Cranbourne's at 22 hearths. The Hearth Tax looked to raise money for the Restoration Government of Charles II through a tax of two shillings on every fireplace (or hearth) in the country to make up for a £200,000 shortfall in the King's revenue. There were 27 annual assessments between the years 1662 and 1689, each with varying degrees of success. Only six assessments survive for Twickenham and Whitton Parish between 1664 and 1674.[7]

Edmund Cooke's will was proved in 1642 and for some reason he was not buried in St Mary's Church, Twickenham. He appears to have disappeared. The last heard of him was on 29 March 1643 when it was recorded in a vestry meeting that his wife Frances should hold the family seat in Whitton for herself and her family. Although assessed for rates in 1642 and 1643, it appears she had moved out by 1644 when the house looks to have remained empty for several years, her name no longer appearing on any further rating lists. Frances died and was buried at St Mary's Church in 1660, having sold her Whitton property seven years earlier to Sir Thomas Mackworth who conveyed it to Henry Kempe Esq., the last known occupant of the house before its purchase by the man whose name the estate bears to this day.

1709 – 1757

Sir Godfrey Kneller

THE EIGHTEENTH CENTURY was Whitton's golden age; a vision of pastoralism and harmony with nature punctuated by classical architecture and attributing adornments; a rural haven close to London. As well as the good and the great, the wealthy and the influential who chose to live here, life was as good for the lower orders of the day ranked as they were about the four highways creating the village epicentre. Work was plentiful in the big houses in the form of service, or on the land and as gardeners, shepherds, cattlemen, builders and labourers.

In 1709, Cooke's mansion was purchased by the greatest master of the English baroque portrait. Gottfried Kniller was born in Lübeck, Germany in 1646 to portrait painter Zacharias Kniller. Godfrey Kneller, as he became known, was originally sent to Leiden University in Holland to study military science, but his love of painting saw him in Amsterdam studying under Rembrandt's pupil, Bol. After travelling through Europe, he arrived in England in 1678 where his talent caught the attention of the Duke of Monmouth, which in turn saw him become Principal Painter to the Court of William and Mary in 1688. He was knighted in 1691 and made a Baronet in 1715, the first painter to be so honoured.

When he first came to London, Kneller lodged with John Banks, a merchant and MP, who rose from relatively humble beginnings to become one of the wealthiest merchants in London and owner of several properties. In 1677, Kneller moved to Durham Yard near Whitehall Palace where he won the valuable patronage of the Duke and Duchess of Monmouth. In 1703, he purchased a house in Great Queen Street, Lincoln's Inn Fields, and married Susanna Grave, daughter of the Reverend John Cawley. From 1711 to 1716, he was governor of the 'Kneller Academy of Painting and Drawing' based on Great Queen Street, the first academy of painting and drawing from life set up in Britain.

It was also in London that Kneller established his workshop-studio with a large team of specialized assistants, many of them foreign, organized for the mass-production of fashionable portraits. Sitters were required only to pose for a drawing of the face, after which various formulas were used to complete the work. It is believed this manufacturing system produced as many as fourteen sitters in a day. Despite this mechanical assembly, Kneller was capable of a much higher quality of work depending on the relationship with the sitter.

Having accumulated a vast amount of wealth, Kneller looked to buy a country house and in 1709 he decided upon Edmund Cooke's house in Whitton, which he promptly enlarged into one described as very stately for the period.[8] Though he worked in London, Kneller would spend the summer months at Whitton where he would entertain his many friends. The only idea we have of the mansion's sumptuous interior are in occasional references. Louis Laguerre was a French decorative painter working in London, primarily decorating the great houses of the nobility. His wall paintings can be found in Blenheim Palace, Marlborough House, Chatsworth and other great houses. Kneller also produced mural paintings for walls and ceilings for such houses, but had Laguerre decorate his own house at Whitton drawn here by Johannes Kip c1715.

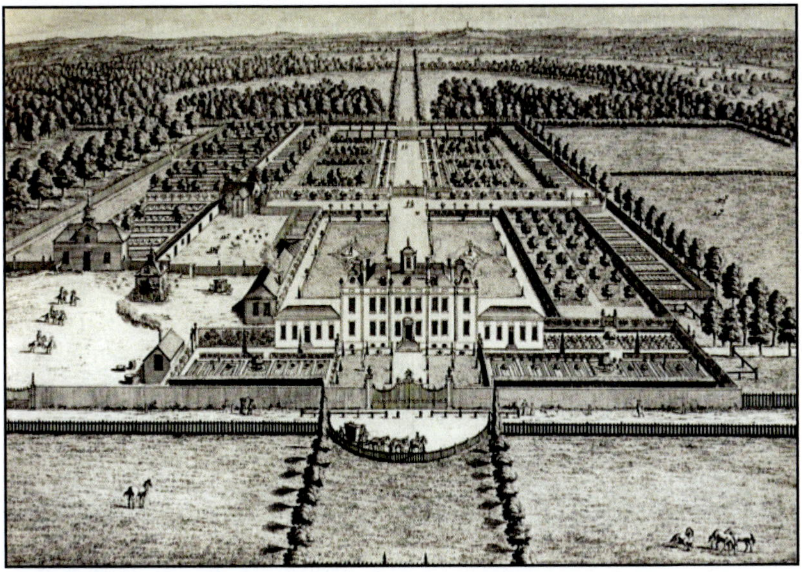

Laguerre was a director of Kneller's Academy and in 1717, when Kneller resigned, he was expected to succeed him but was thwarted by James Thornhill. At the same time, it was agreed that Laguerre should decorate the rebuilt St Paul's Cathedral, only to be ousted again by Thornhill whom Kneller had originally chosen to decorate the staircase of his house in Whitton but when he heard he was turning to portrait painting, thereby competing in the same market, he commissioned Laguerre instead. Sadly, no trace of Laguerre's work at Whitton survives, only a glimpse courtesy of George Vertue, the engraver and antiquary, whose notebooks on British art of the first half of the 18th century provide a valuable source for the period. He writes:

> 'The staircase painted by Laguerre which a fine design represents the arts – cultivated studded with graceful images. The whole being finely drawn and painted being done by the United Judgement of Laguerre and Godfrey Kneller. The poetic description is fine with several allusions to painting.'

As well as the nobility, Kneller also knew most of the leading literary men of his day. With a gift for quick wit and repartee he found himself very much at the centre of the literary world. Thomas Tickell, a minor English poet and man of letters, wrote a poem at Kneller's house in 1722, a year before the painter's death. Entitled 'To Sir Godfrey Kneller at His Country Seat,' it begins:

> *'To Whitton's shades and Hounslow's airy plain,*
>
> *Then Kneller, tak'st thy Summer flight in vain;*
>
> *In vain thy wish give all the rural hours*
>
> *To the fair villa and well-ordered bowers.'*

At Whitton, Kneller was active in local life. He became a Churchwarden of St Mary's, Twickenham in 1713 where he assisted in the rebuilding of the nave after its collapse in April that year. He was a friend of Alexander Pope and as a local JP was noted for some eccentric judgments. Taken ill in London with a fever in May 1722 from which he managed to partially recover, he died the following year at Great Queen Street. He was not buried in his garden at

A glimpse of the house is included in the background of Kneller's self-portrait c1715.

Whitton, as is sometimes suggested, nor in London, but laid to rest in a vault in St Mary's, Twickenham, he had reserved for that purpose. Nor did he equip a large studio at Kneller Hall or leave there 800 or so commissions in various stages of completion following his death.[9]

The estate passed to his widow, Lady Susan, for her lifetime. On her death in 1729, the estate was inherited by Kneller's grandson, Godfrey Kneller Huckle, the product of a liaison Kneller had before his marriage with a Mrs Voss. Together they had a daughter, Agnes. Kneller's heir never lived in Whitton. Having married the heiress to an estate at Donhead in Wiltshire, he chose to live there instead. The Whitton estate was leased out until 1757 when it was sold to Sir Samuel Prime, a prominent London lawyer.

1757 – 1813

The Primes of Whitton Hall

A contemporary pen and ink sketch of Sir Samuel Prime undertaken by George Townshend, 4th Viscount and 1st Marquess Townshend immediately captures the personality vividly portrayed by Twickenham gossipmonger, Laetitia Hawkins, the daughter of Sir John Hawkins, who acted as executor to Dr Johnson and who wrote his biography, only to be outdone by Boswell. Hawkins moved with his family to Twickenham in 1760 where Laetitia accrued volumes of local gossip, anecdotes and memoirs in which she portrayed local residents, including Sir Samuel Prime, whom she describes at some length as: 'a most venerable personage who stood conspicuous. His mode of dress was as grand as it was archaic and, in his figure, and features one of the very grandest. As well as his costume, his wig is afforded much attention.' His voice was 'extremely distinct, grave and sonorous; his enunciation slow, as though eternally claiming the attention of the Speaker in the House of Commons.'[10]

A man of great generosity, Sir Samuel helped set up young men looking for 'a few hundred pounds,' to advance themselves. Hawkins describes Lady Prime as 'a prodigiously fine woman,' not of 'an educated age, but bright, companionable and with a great knowledge of fruit and its cultivation.' Their son, also called Samuel, inherited the estate in 1777 and is described as 'a son who to the last moment of his mother's long protracted life, never relaxed from the most pious and active of filial attention.'

Samuel Prime Junior married Mary Holden and together they raised a large family at Whitton Hall, as the estate was then known, enlarging the house accordingly with an east and west wing. The detached lodge, today the Guardroom at Kneller Hall, occupies the same site as the building depicted by Kip. It was either retained in its original form or rebuilt, but it was in his dramatic alterations to the local landscape that Samuel Prime's signature altered irrevocably the wider Whitton landscape.

In 1780 he purchased the land immediately bordering the southern extent of his property[11] where Lord Belasyse's former mansion obstructed the view from Whitton Hall to the South Downs. Prime demolished the mansion two years later leaving only the kitchen garden, the walls of which survive. Several other houses were demolished in the creation of an extended pleasure ground stretching a quarter of a mile south towards the River Crane and where Kneller Gardens, a public park, is located today.

Edward Ironside was a Supercargo[12] of the Honourable East India Company who collected historical information about Twickenham and published his *History and Antiquities* in 1797. In it he describes Whitton Hall as 'a large well-built brick house, with a handsome front and two wings. The inside is finished with elegance. The staircase, which is large, was painted by Le Guerre (sic). One of the wings is a dining parlour, the other a library. The out offices are extensive and convenient. Mr Prime, since the death of his father, Sir Samuel Prime, has made very considerable alterations, particularly in the gardens and grounds, and enlarged them by additional purchases.'

As evident from a watercolour by William Payne, the front of the house was no longer 'hid as before by high walls and trees,' but now 'very conspicuous,

Watercolour of Whitton Hall by William Payne c1800.

the walls removed, and the whole thrown quite open.' This same arrangement survives but no longer opens 'up a prospect of Surrey and the adjacent country' from the house. The 'handsome lawn to the road, with a coach way around it to the house,' is replaced with a drill ground but still 'guarded by a half-circular range of iron work', with at each end 'two gates with dwarf stone piers, with antique vases on the top.'

'In the gardens to the back,' Ironside concludes, 'is a very fine piece of running water, of considerable extent, over which is thrown a neat wooden bridge. The plantations in all the grounds are considerable and extensive; and there is a gravel walk quite round them, agreeably shaded from the sun in the summer season. The whole of these premises are laid out with great judgement and taste, to the credit of its owner, and with a liberality of spirit peculiar to himself.' With regards to the landscaping of the gardens, Ironside appears unaware that the year before, Whitton Hall had benefited from the fashion of the new gentry in commissioning England's last great landscape gardener whom the experts in these things acknowledge to be the successor to Capability Brown.

1795 – 1796

Humphry Repton

With no real experience of practical horticulture, Humphry Repton became an overnight success due in part to the unique way in which he helped clients visualise his designs. A marketing guru long before such terminology was even considered, his famous Red Books (so called for their binding) came complete with explanatory text and watercolour overlays showing 'before' and 'after' views. Whereas his predecessor Lancelot 'Capability' Brown worked almost exclusively for the wealthiest aristocrats, Repton mostly fine-tuned earlier works, including those of Brown, or won new commissions largely from smaller and newly-founded estates.

Unique among Repton's 400 known commissions are three landscapes traced to the same district. The whereabouts of his Red Book for neighbouring Whitton Park accounting for two of these gardens is unknown. It was sold at auction to a US buyer in 1947 for $9,500.[13] The *Red Book for Whitton Hall*, however, was recently traced to the New York Botanical Garden, one of the world's largest and most important botanical and horticultural research libraries.[14] In a gesture of huge generosity, a scanned copy was provided for the purposes of this publication, and from it we know that Repton surveyed the rear garden at Whitton Hall on 10 December 1795 and completed the Red Book at his Essex home on 7 January 1796. His introduction confirms the Primes had already made changes to the landscape, taking instruction from Repton's best-selling *Sketches and Hints on Landscape Gardening*. Repton's report to Samuel Prime states:

> 'Although the principal object on which you did me the honour to ask my opinion related to the situation and form of a building in the grounds which you considered in other respects as finished, I must thank you for the opportunity given me of showing that the place is capable of further improvement; and as the sketches and maps by which I shall explain my opinion will be thus better preserved I have digested them in my usual manner and hope this small volume will not be deemed unworthy a place in that library, where I am flattered by seeing a copy of my printed work'.

In looking to improve what was essentially a flat, featureless expanse of open ground interrupted by an ornamental lake and plantings, Repton's diplomacy does him credit. 'The neatness of the grounds at Whitton must give pleasure to every admirer of modern gardening who is not a convert to the new and slovenly doctrine of what has been called picturesqueness.' In gently pointing out the landscape's limitations, he continues: 'This delightful spot furnishes the most striking proof that where nature does not produce bold features, or romantic inequalities, yet the mind may be amply gratified with that species of beauty which arises from the combination of wood, lawn, shrubs and water, under the influence of great neatness and order.'

Repton observed that this place enjoyed no natural ruggedness to be trimmed and tamed, but 'a calm and quiet scenery, best calculated for the purposes of man's habitation, but more particularly so for a Gentleman's residence with comfort and elegance.....such is the Character of Whitton.' It required very little improvement to make it 'one of the most pleasant specimens of the powers of Landscape gardening on a situation by nature flat, but not therefore the less beautiful.'

Concentrating on the only creditable feature, Repton saw the 'Outline of the Water' created from the brook flowing through the estate as having the greatest effect when viewed from the rear of the house. Made wider, the addition of boats would give it the semblance of a natural and a navigable river, he ventured. And within this scenario, he proposed a rustic boat house built of logs and thatched to blend in with surrounding foliage so as not to 'shorten the water,' by which he meant not to make the water appear as minor as it actually was. He also suggested a seating area by the boat house commanding a view east over the whole length of water.

In his attempt to create an ornamental lake, Samuel Prime had attempted to divide what Repton describes as 'the copious supply and brilliant colour of the water at Whitton' into two distinct canals. This had the effect of hiding the resultant long island by separating them when viewed from the mansion's rear salon. To remedy this defect at the least expense, excavated earth would be used to fill one channel and create a Ha! Ha!, or sunken fence, that would be hidden from the house, thus softening the bank towards the river.

In looking from the other principal rooms of the house, Repton observed that the water was less conspicuous from the north than that towards the south because it reflected a less brilliant sky. It therefore required to be 'enlivened' by objects 'strongly reflected on its surface.'

As well as the foot bridge leading on and off the island 'illuminated by the western sun,' the siting of an eight-sided Retundo would not only give an appearance of extent and invigorate the landscape with a colour in contrast to the trees and lawn, but also command the best view of the water and the island set between two bridges of different forms. The front arch would present the finest view of the house and lawn, while the arch facing the south east offered an impressive view 'from this high ground looking towards the woods of Richmond Park.'

Samuel Prime died in 1813, his Whitton estate now standing preeminent amongst its former neighbours. Whitton Park, divided and awaiting reunification, was fast fading. The Suckling estate had gradually given way to farming and market gardening, its grand mansion and banqueting hall all but gone, and Lord Belasyse's great house already lost to Samuel Prime Jnr's improvements. The diminution of Whitton as a haunt of grand summer houses

Above: Repton's eight-sided Retundo.
Below: The Rustic Boathouse.

was near complete. Describing the effect his death had on her, local diarist Laetitia Hawkins recalls that Samuel Prime left a family distraught. His eldest daughter replied to Hawkins' first letter of consolation, 'I had hoped that he would have lived till I myself was old.'

Despite his great wealth, Prime's generous settlements to his wife and children was largely managed with the sale of Whitton Hall, which he believed would have proved a burden to his family. Its sale provided a £500 annuity for his wife and £10,000 for his three surviving daughters. His youngest son Richard was bequeathed the house and lands to sell, which he duly did to Charles Calvert MP who had inherited a half-share in a Southwark brewery from his father, who had shot himself in a Cheyne Walk coffee house in 1802.

1813 – 1845

CHARLES CALVERT M.P.

KNOWN AS 'the little brewer' by his political opponents, Charles Calvert looked to bring about a measure of parliamentary reform, declaring that he wanted every county and town in the kingdom to have an equal share in representation. He was elected Whig Member of Parliament for Southwark in 1812, the same year a petition was posted to Parliament for a Private Enclosure Act for Twickenham Parish.

Two thirds of land had by this time been enclosed over a long period of time, often piecemeal by common agreement or formal document and sometimes by unlawful encroachment of common land.

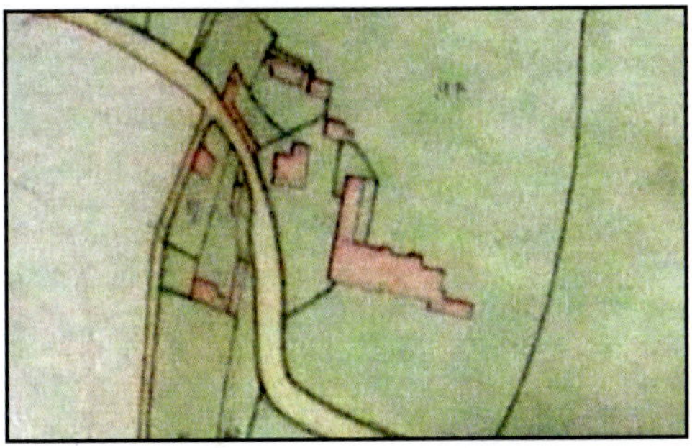

The Commissioners for Twickenham appointed to determine all claims were sworn in on 6 July 1813. When their work was proclaimed complete and finalised in September 1817, 16 acres were allotted to Calvert under the Enclosure Award, bringing the Kneller Hall holdings to 77 acres. This extract of the 1818 Enclosure Plan shows the mansion extensively remodeled by Philip Hardwick, the architect principally associated with railway stations and warehouses. As well as a 'noble' drawing room, 'spacious' dining room and 85 feet conservatory to the front, the plan shows the addition of a servant block striking north off the west wing, which survives to this day.

In 1822, at the age of 54, Calvert married the 17-year-old 'pretty gipsy daughter of Sir William Rowley,' who bore him a child 'within eight months.' Ten years later and after an active career in Parliament where he presented anti-slavery petitions and spoke in favour of allowing Thames watermen to ply their trade on Sundays, Calvert died intestate, leaving his partners to pay off all his debts and secure the principal part of his property for his family, including an infant heir. Calvert's widow and two of their children filed a bill in favour of the proposal. The freehold estate was ordered by the court to be sold with the sale of the copyhold estate dependent on the number of creditors remaining unsatisfied.[15]

In 1836, the new Poor Law Commission for Twickenham assessed Jane Calvert for a Mansion, Ground & Lodge at £305 and with 23 acres of land at £71.[16] Three years later the High Court of Chancery directed the sale of the freehold estate and the money arising placed into a bank partly for the benefit of the infant defendant, Charles Calvert junior, as customary heir and trustee of his father's copyholds in Isleworth Syon, Isleworth Rectory and Twickenham. Under an order dated 11 June 1841, the Kneller Hall Estate was put up for auction.

A Miss Watson successfully bid £9,450, only to immediately object to the title and request to be discharged from the sale. Under a decree from a Court, as in this instance, and where a material error could be proved as to that decree, the Court was duty bound to comply. And because the Court had no authority to sell the estate of an infant, the purchaser was not duty bound to wait for the error to be corrected. Miss Watson was discharged from her purchase in 1843 and granted the stock arising from the investment of the purchase money to be paid into court minus tax, her costs, charges and expenses incurred in respect of the purchase, including the cost of the petition. While the money retained by the auctioneer was to be repaid to her, she was ordered to give up possession and account for any rent received.

The auction catalogue has the extent of the estate amounting to over 102 acres, which included the 25 acres purchased by Samuel Prime to improve the view from the house. The whole is described as 'most eligibly situated only eleven miles from London, in a beautiful part of the County of Middlesex, being at Whitton, a short distance from Twickenham and in the parishes of Isleworth and Twickenham.'[17]

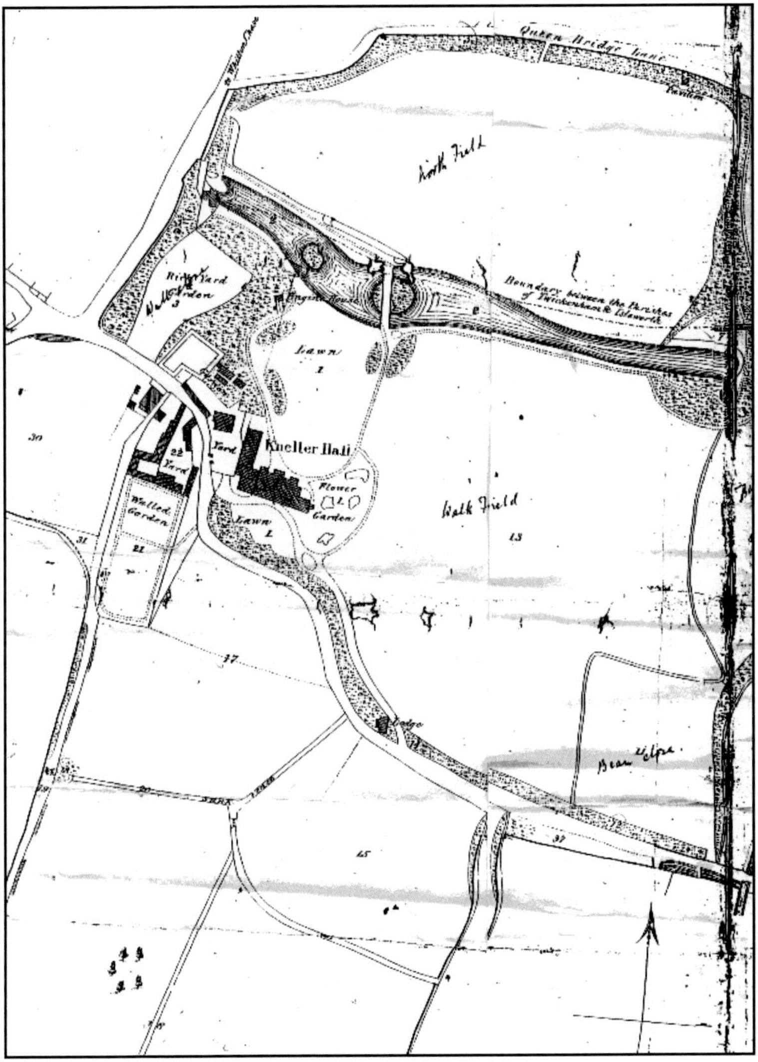

Extent of the Kneller Hall Estate 1841.

This 'highly improvable estate' came 'replete with every accommodation appropriate for the occupation of any family of the first distinction, most pleasantly situated in park-like Grounds, with all the appendages of Ornamental Pleasure Grounds, Beautiful Lake, Luxuriant Plantations, Lawn, Parterres, Walks of great variety, Conservatory, Grapery, Greenhouse, Entrance Lodge, a Good Farm House and Homestead; Gardener's Cottage, a well enclosed Kitchen Garden and sundry Parcels of Rich Meadow Land, containing about seven Acres of highly productive Arable and Garden Ground.'

A richly planted ribbon of ornamental trees and shrubs enclosed the grounds and with the southern planting extending east of Chase Bridge as far west to Whitton Dean (as it was then spelt). About half way, the main entrance was via a new set of ornamental piers along Kneller Road that remain, flanked by a tidy new lodge that doesn't.

The sole survivor of the paved courtyard complex across the road from today's Guardhouse is the Duke of Cambridge public house. The green open space we see today then hosted a brick and tiled complex including stables for six horses and six carriages; a harness room; granary and brew house. Attaching this service yard was The Homestead (since demolished), a comfortable farmhouse that later became known as The Croft. The walled enclosure surviving today was then a well-stocked kitchen garden.

The specifications of 'the capital and noble mansion' laid out in the auction catalogue exposes much of Kneller's original arrangement, except for an 85-feet centrally-heated conservatory elaborating the frontage. This allowed for traditional entrance to the main house from the Carriage Drive and communication between Calvert's additional dining and drawing room extensions.

The 'capital entrance hall' measuring 25ft by 19ft was unchanged since Kneller's day with its 'spacious and principal staircase' ornamented with wainscoted balustrades flanked by walls beneath a ceiling painted not by Sir Godfrey Kneller 'or some of his pupils,' as the survey has it, but by Laguerre. This flight of stairs led to a boudoir with a handsome carved chimney piece and ornamental ceiling comprising four relief medallions and a rich cornice; a morning room boasting a paneled ceiling and statuary chimney piece. As well as day and sleeping nurseries, there were seven bedrooms, two anti-rooms, three dressing rooms and a water closet. A secondary staircase led to the upper floor where there were six servants' apartments and a water closet. The basement comprised arched wine cellars; a knife store; a 'bottle apartment' and various ale and beer cellars.

Calvert's additions comprised a 'most splendid and lofty drawing room' with ceiling and cornice picked out in gold and with a carved statuary chimney piece decorated with scagliola Corinthian columns and pilasters. Measuring 40ft by 26ft, its footprint corresponds with the east wing of the current building, although much altered. The 'noble dining room measuring 32ft by 21ft' corresponds precisely with the lower level museum space comprising the west wing. Elements on the ground level may still survive in part from Calvert's improvements such as the 'Bow Breakfast Room' with ante-room; a gentlemen's room complete with its own water closet and another small ante-room; a bedroom and a study.

Given the evidence of its arrangement shown in the 1818 Enclosure Award Plan, the service block extending north from the west wing contained the housekeeper's room; the butler's pantry; the second footman's room; two large closets set beneath two store rooms along the corridor; the servants' hall; a 'capital' kitchen, scullery, 'a good water closet' and pantry.

Stepping out into the rear grounds provided a choice of walks. Taking the gravel path left of the lawn, a series of shrubberies hid the utilitarian wood yard with its tiled shed and brick and slated carpenter's workshop. There was a melon yard enclosed in a high brick wall; a greenhouse, grapery, forcing house and potting shed. Looming high above an ice well and a mushroom house was a 'large and lofty brick-built tower called the Water House' that stood three stories high and from where water was pumped from a natural spring to a spacious cistern to supply water under pressure to the mansion and to a brick and slated bath house. A short walk along the banks of the impressive lake was Repton's Rustic Boat House.

Taking the path east of the 'tastefully disposed Lawn,' a flower garden briefly diverted attention from the 14-acre Walk Field we partly recognise today as the sports field. Moving north towards plantations 'in the highest state of perfection and luxuriancy, laid out to produce the most beautiful effect,' was the lake, 'beautiful and extensive.' Repton's twin bridges led from one side of the Islet to the other connecting the 11-acre North Field in Isleworth Parish. Thereafter a shady route skirted the northern extent of the grounds adjacent to Queen's Bridge Lane, now the eastern arm of Whitton Dene. Central to this promenade was The Pavilion and the full appreciation of Repton's landscape punctuated with 'picturesque Groups of Trees scattered about the Park-like Grounds.'

Other parcels of land included either plantations or meadow, mostly rented out. The eastern extent of the estate boundary is broadly defined in today's terms by Spray Lane, the footpath linking Kneller Road and Whitton Dene. Then it followed a more circuitous route navigating a complex series of boundaries along the Duke of Northumberland's river in the form of two footpaths, both convoluted. The one between today's sports field and the river circumnavigated a 2-acre rectangular anomaly known as Bean Close before striking north to roughly take the line of where Spray Lane enters Whitton Dene today. The other route ran from where Spray Lane joins Kneller Road east across today's Cardinal Vaughn Memorial School playing field. The rest of the Estate's land extended east across the southern third of the Rugby Football Union's west field to a ribbon of land represented today by the South Stand boundary and Whitton Road. All the timber on the land had been carefully valued by the auctioneers at £1,866 in addition to the purchase price. A 'fair price' was also expected for the shrubs and plants in the conservatory and hothouses. Included in the price, however, were the clock (presumably the same or similar to that atop of today's Guardroom); the brewery utensils and other fixtures and fittings in and about the mansion and other premises.

1845 – 1850

A Pauper Palace

TWENTY-SEVEN YEARS HAD passed since the Enclosure Award had removed the last vestiges of Common and Waste Lands benefiting the likes of Charles Calvert and their ambitions. In that time huge shifts in the fortunes of Twickenham parish had taken place. One-tenth contributions, or Tithes, historically paid in kind either to a religious order or as a government tax, were still payable across the majority of English parishes. In 1836, economic reformers successfully steered the Tithe Commutation Bill through Parliament, but it wasn't until 1844 that a voluntary agreement was reached in Twickenham parish. To avoid any unnecessary expense, the same maps prepared for the 1818 Enclosure Award were adapted for the new survey. Of the several landowners that had already acquired Tithes chargeable on their lands was the Calvert holdings in Whitton at 84 acres, worth five pounds and five shillings. Jane Calvert continued living in the house until her death in 1845, the year John Maurice Herbert, barrister and Assistant Tithe Commissioner, endorsed the Tithe Award for Twickenham parish.

The corrected plan was prepared by local land surveyor and draughtsman, W T Warren. When it was published in 1846[18] much of the Kneller Hall Estate was in the hands of Morris Emmanuel Esq., one of ten men who owned just over half the land in the parish.[19] Emmanuel was a passionate supporter of the Reform Bill and a staunch advocate for all men to have the right to vote. He believed in free education and would discuss with his friend and self-proclaimed reformer Louis Kyezor the future of Whitton based on the coming of the railway. The number of people living in Whitton at this time was around 450. The 16 individuals described in the 1841 census as being of independent means would have provided regular work for the 218 males and 232 females, minus the seasonal agricultural labourers over-crowding the mean cottages largely comprising the hamlet. With all the grand estates bar Kneller Hall and Whitton Park crumbling along with their influences, the two

Jewish businessmen saw an opportunity to turn this neglected place into a thriving enclave attracting a better class of citizen.[20]

Pauper children received between 30 and 40 per cent of poor law relief in nineteenth-century Britain. Thus, their impact on that resource where illiteracy further lessened the slim chances of children born into poverty was substantial. The government was looking at alternatives to the workhouse by placing the most deprived children in schools that promised a basic education, regular meals and a level of healthcare. Pauper Palaces, as they were dubbed, sought to turn 'pauper and criminal children' into able and employable citizens. Often housed in magnificent surroundings, albeit taking the form of barracks, vocational training for boys took the form of tailoring, cobbling or as blacksmiths. Girls were trained in household occupations. Within this framework Kneller Hall was acquired by the Council of Education after the death of Morris Emmanuel in 1847.

When it opened in 1850, the Kneller Hall Teacher Training College was experimental, looking to service a new construct known as District Pauper Schools.[21] The Rev. Dr. Frederick Temple was appointed Principal. His deputy was Francis Turner Palgrave who while at Kneller Hall would visit Tennyson, who was living in Twickenham. The two men remained great friends for many years and it was during a holiday spent together that Palgrave's popular anthology *Golden Treasury* of English poetry, songs and lyrics came about, still published in regular new editions under his name. Less successful, however, was the educational venture he and Temple had embarked upon at Kneller Hall to train teachers to then work in District Pauper Schools.

Almost immediately it met with failure, not because of poor management, but because the new concept of District Pauper Schools never actually materialised. Kneller Hall became purposeless. Dr. Temple, who later went on to become Archbishop of Canterbury, was called before a Parliamentary committee to explain the origin and history of the ill-fated institution.[22] He was unable to answer how many schoolmasters had been trained. And because there were no more than half a dozen pauper schools for them to go to, the majority of the few students attending the school went on to teach in

Rev. Dr Frederick Temple.

J F Palgrave.

workhouse schools, some to the Colonies and others to teach in prisons. The chairman of the committee asked if there was any difference in the training at Kneller Hall from the system pursued at other training schools. Dr Temple answered that it was a little more formal and more regulated, but otherwise much the same as in any other. He was unable to tell how much the training cost at Kneller Hall, only that it was very high because the school never reached its full potential. Asked if the training exceeded £50 a head, Temple answered 'considerably.' It was a very large place with extensive grounds. For the first year there were only ten students. It was a very expensive experiment.

The original contract was £17,336, exclusive of fittings, but the total cost came in at £40,000, equivalent to over £5 million pounds in today's terms. To a design by architect George Mair based on Woollaton Hall near Nottingham, the effect of the new frontage was declared most satisfactory. As we see it today, the cornices; parapets; quoins; dressings to the windows, and other enrichments, except for a small portion of the arcade worked in cement, were of Bath stone. The plinth round the building was of Portland stone and the

REFERENCES TO PLAN.

SERVANTS' DEPARTMENT.

A—Steam-engine room, &c.
B—Wash-house.
C—Laundry.
D—Drying-room.
E—Knives, shoes, &c.
F—Coals, wood, &c.
G—Store.
H—Covered way.
I—Store-room.
K—Weighing-room.
L—Tradesmen's entrance.
M—Scullery.
N—Kitchen.
O—Housekeeper's room.
P—Ditto store-closet.
Q—Way to larder, dairy, &c., under class-room.

SCHOOL DEPARTMENT.

R—Dining-hall.
S—Corridor.
T—Pupils' stairs to dormitories.
U—Class-rooms.
V—School library, and reception-room.
W—Ambulatory, with glass roof.
X—Pupils' stairs to chapel over library.
Y—Entrance to reception-room.
Z—Areas.
1—Urinaries.
2—Bath-room.
3—Day wash-hand room.

THE PRINCIPAL'S RESIDENCE.

4—Hall and staircase.
5—Dining-room.
6—Library.
7—Entrance for tradesmen to servants' offices.

N.B. A clothes-brushing room and shoes-cleaning room for pupils are under the dining-hall, R.

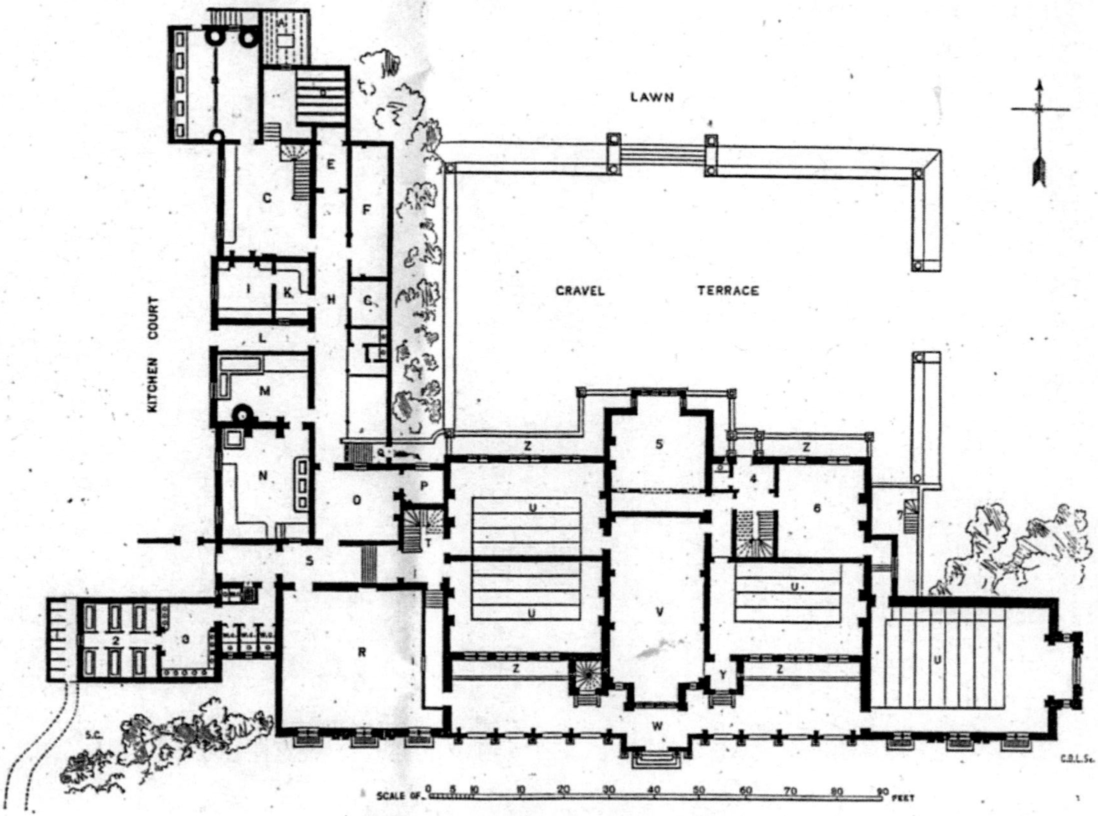

GROUND PLAN OF KNELLER HALL TRAINING-SCHOOL.

external walls faced with red brick with the whole in the ‘neo-Jacobethan’ style.[23]

Its 17 bays split into five recessed, or projecting ranges with the stained–glass centre bay the widest, are set between two square pavilion towers forming the left and right bays, each crowned by a stone and leaded cupola. The drawing and dining rooms added by Calvert were refaced and raised to carry a two-storey dormitory extension. The servants' block was retained, modified and enlarged to provide accommodation for 100 pupils equipped with dwarf partitions six feet six inches high to form individual dormitories of about seven feet by twelve feet and each with its own toilet.[24]

The class-rooms were fitted with desks on raised platforms. The handsome chapel surviving intact to this day was placed over the school library in the form of a double-volume chamber on the first floor with a gallery on the second occupying the remaining height of the building. Its unassumingly decorated plain wooden furnishings sit beneath a wooden ceiling supported by carved brackets, the whole enhanced by the imposing window that probably featured clear glass when first constructed.

THE KNELLER HALL TRAINING SCHOOL, WHITTON.

As well as apartments for three masters, there was a separate residence for the Principal at ground level, which, together with the school library and three adjoining class-rooms comprised the space formerly occupied by Kneller's original house. Some of the columns of the former drawing-room were transferred to the new principal lecture-room. Otherwise, the interior accommodation was carried out without decoration to 'render the whole of the arrangements as complete as possible, both regards economy of labour and expense in execution.'

A three-horse power steam-engine was employed to pump water from the estate's wells to tanks and cisterns on the roof, as well as to power machinery for washing in the laundry department where a mangle was turned by steam. As well as supplying heat to a drying-closet, the engine also supplied hot water to the kitchen and for bathing. The building was lit by gas, supplied through a main laid down from Twickenham by the Brentford Gas-light Company. There was central heating, the ground-floor and staircases warmed by furnaces in the vaulted basement throughout the central portion of the building. The boundary wall complete with its 18th century dwarf piers and the detached servants' offices (now the Guardhouse) survived this comprehensive reconstruction, whereas the whole of Kneller's house was demolished with no undue consternation, deemed as it was to be devoid of any architectural character worthy of note externally or internally, 'being merely a plain square brick dwelling-house, two stories in height, with red brick arches over the external openings.'[25]

The only (visible) trace of Kneller's house, apart from 18th century limestone paving to parts of the cellar floor, is the foundation stone removed from the north-east corner of the house during demolition. It bears the inscription: 'The building of this House was begun by Sir Godfrey Kneller, Bart., A.D. 1709.' Its last recorded whereabouts was as an exhibit in Radnor House, Twickenham, when the local museum was established there between the wars. Radnor House was destroyed in a bombing raid during the Second World War and many of the artifacts went missing, including Kneller's foundation stone. However, during the course of researching this account, it was discovered nestling in the fireplace of the Officers' mess, unrecognised and uncelebrated; its inscription cut short by the effect of the enemy bomb that returned it home.

1854 – 1914

Reveille

Legend has it in 1854, at the time of the Crimean War, a military parade held in Turkey to celebrate Queen Victoria's birthday saw around 20 British Army bands combine in a performance of the national anthem. The custom at this time was for regiments to hire civilian bandmasters, each of whom had free rein. The resulting performance on this occasion was nothing short of an embarrassing and humiliating cacophony. Back home, meanwhile, the Royal Engineers on staff of the London District were grappling with the problem of billeting the Guards stationed in the capital. A decision made to build a new barracks in Chelsea alongside the Royal Hospital was halted due to the lack of space for a drill ground. Then, in 1856, the Royal Military Asylum in Chelsea caught the eye of the War Department.

This was a charitable institution for the children of soldiers that was founded by the Duke of York in 1801, which to later generations became known as the Duke of York's Royal Military School. It stands in the spacious grounds that today comprise a chic shopping centre off the King's Road. Deemed eminently suitable to convert into the much-needed barracks, the children could be moved elsewhere. For instance, it had come to the attention of the War Department that the Council of Education had on its hands a large building in Twickenham, known as Kneller Hall where the squeal of children's voices was already a familiar sound emanating from a sectioned-off piece of its grounds west of the newly-refurbished grand mansion standing empty.

Some children from Whitton had access to education with the opening of Archdeacon Cambridge School, Twickenham, in 1842, which was a two-mile walk away. In 1853, the parish of Holy Trinity, Twickenham, came together with the consent of Dr Temple to grant Whitton its own school to be built into the grounds of Kneller Hall. In keeping with the spirit of the place, St Philip and St James school was 'to be forever appropriated and used as a school for the education of children and adults, or children only of the labouring, manufacturing and other poorer classes of the District.'[26]

Sunk into the walled enclosure of the estate's former melon yard, the school was 'open and fairly well ventilated on the south and west sides, but closely bounded by the grounds of Kneller Hall on the north and east.' The playground was deemed to be of 'insufficient size and neither paved nor drained.' The school building fronting onto Kneller Road was 'fairly well built with red brick facings, stone dressings and slated roofs.' It was also 'fairly well lighted and ventilated and heated by means of open fireplaces.' The height of the rooms and the size of classrooms were 'satisfactory.' Passages and entrances were 'convenient' and of sufficient size and separate for each department. What eventually became known as 'The Whitton Schools,' survived until the 1960s when it was demolished, leaving only the profile of its intrusion as a poorly healed wound in the side of Kneller Hall's boundary wall.

In June 1856, the Treasury wrote to the War Department confirming its intention to convert Kneller Hall into a Training School and Asylum. Precisely how the estate came into the equation is clear from the 1845 *Plan for Twickenham Parish* prepared by W.T. Warren of Isleworth, who also happened to be Land Surveyor and Draughtsman to H.R.H the Duke of Cambridge, Commander-in-Chief of the British Army and one of the Asylum Commissioners. Although having agreed in principle to the move of the Asylum from Chelsea to Whitton, there was the embarrassment keenly felt over the poor quality of British military bands, as opposed to their French counterparts whose excellence was attributed to a government-endorsed Army School of Music.[27]

Cambridge had studied music as part of his education and valued the quality of his former bandmaster, Henry Schallehn, a civilian, when commanding the 17th Lancers.

Schallehn had long argued for the necessity of improving the position of bandmasters and bandsmen to reach the standard of continental bands. One of his associates was James Smyth, bandmaster of the Royal Artillery Band, who drafted a proposal for the establishment of an Army School of Music that was conveyed to Cambridge. Thus, Kneller Hall offered a real opportunity to move that ideal forward in favour of relocating of the Chelsea asylum.

In August 1856, Schallehn circulated a treatise on the subject entitled *The British Military College of Music* with the object of creating a school designed to supply trained musicians for the Army and Navy. It was no longer acceptable for musicians in these services to leave for better pay in civilian life once they had been trained at public expense, he argued. The establishment of a college would increase competition and opportunities for advancement, as it was on the continent. The great advantage of such an institution would be that all musicians across both services would be trained as one.

The plan initially involved the reception of soldiers and sailors selected by their commanding officers, and for the sons of those men who had exhibited the same musical aptitude. All would receive a thorough and practical knowledge of music with a higher level of tuition available to those looking to become bandmasters. Kneller Hall was already fitted out for 90 students 'on a very liberal scale of accommodation.' This number could be more than doubled with the removal of the wooden partitions installed for the Teachers' Training School educational and other 'minor alterations and additions,' totaling a further £33,000.[28] Such a substantial sum was not readily available to the Treasury at the time and so it looked ahead to the 1857–8 budget to provide for the establishment of a Military School of Music that would save the country money and enhance its reputation abroad.

Given the eye-watering amount of funding required, every regiment was required to pay a subscription of five guineas for every three musicians supplied. Non-paying regiments were subject to an 'adequate fee' for every pupil taken. A preliminary outlay of £500–£600 would be required for musical instruments, and with around £1,000 per annum to fund the scheme, including a Director's salary, professors' fees, repairs and other expenses. With his Royal Highness expecting favourable opinions on this subject, the scheme was set to proceed.

All candidates would be of exemplary character and possess some musical ability. Those intending to qualify for Bugle or Trumpet Majors would need to have acquired a good knowledge of the instrument. Candidates for those looking to become Bandmasters would be those deemed by their Commanding Officer to have sufficient musical knowledge and general intelligence. The object of the exercise was to emulate the celebrated Ecole Militaire Musicale in Paris to perform as a single unit in harmony.

On 10 November 1856, the Commander Royal Engineers, London District, notified the Inspector General of Fortifications that suitable accommodation could be found in the West Wing of Kneller Hall without incurring any extra expense. By 11 December, the transfer of the estate to the War Department was complete. The Education Department wrote to announce, 'on Monday 5th January 1857, the Revd. Frederick Temple, late Principal of Kneller Hall, will be on the premises there authorised and ready to deliver up possession thereof to the officer whom the Secretary of State for War may authorise to receive the same.'[29]

Cambridge had decided on Henry Schallehn as musical director on a salary of £350 a year. He had already drawn up estimates to cover the cost of instruments, which came in at a worrying £200 above expectations. He was allotted the two sitting rooms and two bedrooms with a corridor between on the second floor, previously occupied by the Rev. Temple. Schallehn's assistant, Mr Mandel, was assigned a bedroom and a sitting room on the third floor. Thanks to the recollections of an unknown boy soldier sent to Kneller Hall from the Canterbury Cavalry Depot in 1859,[30] we learn that the School initially possessed only one instrument of each type and students had to make do with what they were given.

They slept two to a dormitory with Reveille at 6am, followed by 'a walk in the country' until 7.30, with breakfast at 8. Band practice was from 9 to 12.30 with lunch at 1 o'clock. The afternoon practice session was from 2 to 4.30 in the summer. Tea was at 5 with evening band practice until 7pm when the instruments were locked up for the night. On the staff were four Professors of Music assisting Schallehn in providing a thorough practical knowledge as well as the theory of music and the art of arranging for bands. Also, sufficient instruction was to be given in French, Italian and German in order to understand the terminology employed by European composers.

Professor of Theory was Charles Mandeville, described as a 'painstaking and clever teacher' who gave two lectures a week. Professor Zeiss was a hard taskmaster for cornet and trumpet, whereas Professor Sullivan taught clarinet and trombone with a ready smile and jokes. His more famous son, Arthur, was not born at Kneller Hall, as is sometimes suggested, but some years later at Sandhurst where his father became Bandmaster at the Royal Military College. As well as Professor Hanks of the Royal Italian Opera, there was Mr. Cioffi, 'a marvellous performer on the slide trombone who lined his silk hat with newspaper cuttings of his performances.'

On 10 February 1857, instructions were issued for 'the parties composing the Military Music Class' to proceed from their several Regiments to arrive at their new posting on the 17th or as soon thereafter as possible.[31] Lt. Col. H S Stephens was selected as Commandant, albeit briefly. With full kit, but without instruments, the company was to be recognised as a regular detachment of troops subject to the usual regulations regarding reveille, tattoo, messing and passes etc. The initial music class assembled at Kneller Hall on 3 March 1857.

Following his visit, the Duke of Cambridge wrote in October that he was satisfied with what he had seen and that the object of the exercise was being realised. There were 100 pupils under instruction with 30 or 40 more due to join. Such was his confidence in the overall outcomes of the scheme that he felt compelled to increase the subscriptions from £8 to £10. Writing again in June 1858 he looked to the Secretary of State for War to raise the status of successful students at the Military School of Music, Kneller Hall, as the establishment was called for the first time.

The student band played in the grounds of Kneller Hall for two afternoons a week, when visitors were welcome to come and listen. But the shortage of instruments and the quality of some of the students chosen to be sent there, as well as the behaviour of some Bandmasters, left something to be desired. Henry Schallehn himself failed to come up to expectations. Described as 'great showman, somewhat voluble and something of a charlatan,' he was dismissed from Kneller Hall in 1859 and succeeded by his assistant, Carl Mandel.

Personally intervening, the Duke of Cambridge proposed that regiments placed orders for instruments from more than one provider directly through

Kneller Hall, thus eliminating financially dubious agreements with Bandmasters in the purchase of musical instruments on pain of instant dismissal. His Royal Highness also had concerns about the medical fitness of some of the students selected to attend Kneller Hall, requiring all soldiers, especially boys, to undergo a thorough medical examination before attending. The school was not there to teach the rudiments of music. Students were to be drawn from Regimental Bands 'for the inculcation of the highest principles of the science.'

By 1870 it was becoming clear that the Regimental Bands' remit extended beyond their important role in the day to day life of the Army. The standard of performance generated by the work at Kneller Hall was starting to attract the attention of the civilian world. As such, the government began to relieve the regiments of some of the financial burden on them, and by Royal Warrant extended an annual grant of £80 to the Regimental Band Fund. On 1 April 1876, the government assumed entire financial responsibility for the School.

Against such heroic backdrops as Rorke's Drift; General Robert's march on Kanda in Afghanistan and Woolsey's occupation of Cairo, in the little-known hamlet of Whitton in West Middlesex the British Army's Military School of Music celebrated the 25th anniversary of its formation, its aims and objectives achieved. What lay ahead was continued improvement and excellence in all that it served to do.

The band seldom performed away from Kneller Hall, only once a year giving a public performance at St Paul's Cathedral. By 1882 the Wednesday afternoon concerts were well established, highly popular and well attended. These 'At Homes,' as they were called, were held on the lawn at half-past three in May and September and at four o'clock during the other summer months. The *British Bandsman* magazine offers a familiar depiction of this popular event a century and more later.[32]

> 'The last Venetian Fete of the season was held at the Royal Military School of Music on 21st September and despite the unpleasant weather, attracted a large number of visitors, not a few of whom had travelled from Town. The illuminations were as effective as ever. Hundreds of

lamps bounded the lake upon which were pleasure craft, and many lesser lights surrounded the platform, the general scene being one of brilliance.

'Music was dispensed by the Band of 150 performers. The programme was in many respects similar to that of previous Fetes and introduced several descriptive pieces, glees and part songs. The orchestral portion of the programme met with full appreciation, the strings being manipulated with skill and efficiency.

'The Concert terminated with a Grand Tattoo, commencing with the Evening Gun and introducing First Post, Slow and Quick March, Doubling, the hymn 'Abide with Me', the National Anthem and finally the Second Post sounded by Bugles. Much applause greeted the performers, who looked very picturesque in their varied uniforms, illuminated by coloured lamps and the flash of a Search Light.

'The Kneller Hall Fetes will no doubt form an attractive feature of future summer entertainments in the district.'

The Graphic was a weekly illustrated newspaper that prided itself on the superior quality of its engravings, devoting much attention to literature, arts, sciences, the fashionable world, sport, music, royal occasions and national celebrations and ceremonials. The September 1894 issue reported on the no-less impressive full band practice at Kneller Hall where the magazine's reporter recalled 'not so very long ago, the army tradition was enough to have long hair and to speak broken English to be the Bandmaster of a British regiment.'[33] Where there was then a 'least flattering exhibition of British Military music,' now regimental bands, 'both at home and on colonial and Indian service,' were things to be proud of; 'and not a little of this improvement due to the teachings of Kneller Hall. There are one or two things nowadays which are managed rather better than in the good old times.....and one of them is our military music.'

Practice of the full band when the weather was bad took place in a room barely able to accommodate them, which caused *The Graphic* to couch a familiar contemporaneous criticism that the mansion itself is 'much better suited to the needs of a gentle-man's private dwelling-house than to those of a public institution.' However, the sound was considered to be 'splendid, and the sight of the band thus practicing is in itself very interesting.' Of the most accomplished performers was 'a black soldier of the Queen from Lagos.'

On Sunday mornings, a large number of listeners from 'many places round about' were allowed to gather on the front lawn to hear the music emanating from the chapel where a service was held 'the like of which can be heard nowhere else in the kingdom.' The 'resounding music' of the 150-strong band was joined by the mustel organ[34] and choir of 40 voices. 'It is a volume of sound with which the tiny chapel seems to throb and tremble.....Such was the overpowering effect of that magnificent thunderous harmony.'

Frank Dadd's illustration accompanying *The Graphic*'s report indicates a very distinct type of musically inclined local inhabitant who attended the concerts, as opposed to a later postcard view that provides a very different perspective on Kneller Hall's relationship with its closest and less affluent neighbours.

In this postcard view, three boys are photographed skulking on the culvert directing Whitton's brook along Whitton Dean[35] and into the grounds of

Kneller Hall. Superficially, it means little beyond an interesting view of the landscape as it looked around the turn of the last century. However, the boundary stone pictured west of the brook is key to this scenario where one boy stands centre stream with his back to the photographer; another sits facing the camera with a rueful glare at the offending stone and a third sullenly rests against the War Department's wooden fence.

The backdrop to this scene dates back to February 1884 when the Royal Engineers Office requested permission from the Heston and Isleworth Local Board to enclose the brook with wooden fencing. The object of the exercise was to stop to locals washing their horses, carts and sheep between this point and the former mill pond. The Local Board refused the War Department permission on the grounds there was a proven public right of way and as such was powerless to act. Adjudicating, the Treasury Solicitor pronounced that shifting the fence and clarifying the boundary were distinct from each other. The War Department may have appeared to have acquired the strip of land between the stream and the pond, but it wasn't proven.[36]

In July, estimates were sought for additional boundary stones to define ownership of what was deemed to be 'waste land.' The Ordnance Survey Map prepared for the War Department to define the extent of the Kneller Hall Estate shows how much the ornamental lake had deteriorated due to the amount of waste entered into it. The western half had narrowed into a boggy marshland. Repton's bridges crossed a fragment of the original breadth. What water continued to flow reverted to a narrow canal feeding the eastern half of the lake's original form. The map plots all of the War Department's proposed and existing boundary stones set into walls and the centre line of roads and centre-stream of Whitton Brook.

There were two classes of scholars attending Kneller Hall; band boys sent from their regiments between the ages of 14 and 19 known as pupils, and young sergeants looking to qualify as Bandmasters known as students. The pupils stayed from 18 months to two years, depending on their capacity to learn. The students remained for longer periods. While at Kneller Hall both groups were under full military discipline and regulations. One curious feature of the dormitories noted by *The Graphic* was that the boys were grouped together according to the instruments they played, and their rooms named accordingly. For example, the 'E Flat Clarionet Room' and the 'French Horn Passage.' Euphoniums and trombones lodged together. The walls of the rooms were adorned with educational posters such as 'Scale for the Clarionet' and Theory of the French Horn.' When the boys were not engaged in band practice they were generally to be found in their rooms 'solemnly tootling on their appointed instruments.'[37]

The sergeant students were expected as part of their duties to assist in the teaching of the pupils under the supervision of the masters. The students lodged and messed away from the pupils in a typical sergeants' mess complete with a good library (of musical works) and opportunities 'for less professional recreation.' There were 120 pupils and 50 students, which comprised the band of 82 reed instruments; 57 brass together with percussion and spring basses playing music which, according to the writer, 'a few years ago we only expected to hear at St. James's Hall or at the Crystal Palace.'

Each evening, the band went through a programme of eight pieces, the chief feature of which was a suite, or one of the symphonies arranged for a military band by one of the students or one of the bandmasters. Besides these were overtures and selections and frequently a march composed by one of the more creative students. Overall, the experience presented a 'fine, and splendid entertainment alike to the ear and to the imagination, for the band gathered together from so many parts of the Empire contains the promise, if not the pick, of the army.'

Elsewhere, Parliament had abolished the custom of officers selling their commissions when they retired, a resentment the Duke of Cambridge shared with most other officers. His strongest ally in the Music School enterprise had been his cousin, Queen Victoria, whom, despite bestowing the prefix 'Royal' on his Military School of Music in August 1887, was also keen on reform. Several campaigners and leading generals opposed to the Duke banded together, eager to replace him. Forced to resign in November 1895, he dutifully carried out his annual inspection of Kneller Hall that same year, the final act of his great 40-year endeavour in which he steered its advance into the important musical institution it had become.

With it moving from strength to strength, accommodation at Kneller Hall was becoming stretched. A substantial number of student bandsman, their wives and children were impacting heavily on an already overcrowded and meagre local housing stock. In 1861 the population of Whitton stood at 604. The arrival of the Military Music School boosted that figure to 729. In 1871 the number of students and pupils rose to 140, advancing the local population to 893. In 1881 the number had risen to 177 with a civilian population of 710. The number attending the School decreased slightly in 1891 to 169, while the Whitton population increased by 58 to 768 forcing the War Department to consider purpose-built accommodation for its married students. The site selected was that within the walls of Lord Belasyse's former garden to the south west of Kneller Hall, but still part of the estate with a right of way leading into the enclosure alongside the Duke of Cambridge public house.[38]

Erected between 1892 and 1894 at a cost of £5,785, the Married Quarters consisted of a three-storey block built of red brick with a tiled roof and four entrances facing west, away from Kneller Hall. Each of the eight ground floor units consisted of a living room, a scullery and one bedroom. The same for the first floor. The attic comprised a further 12 bedrooms for single men.

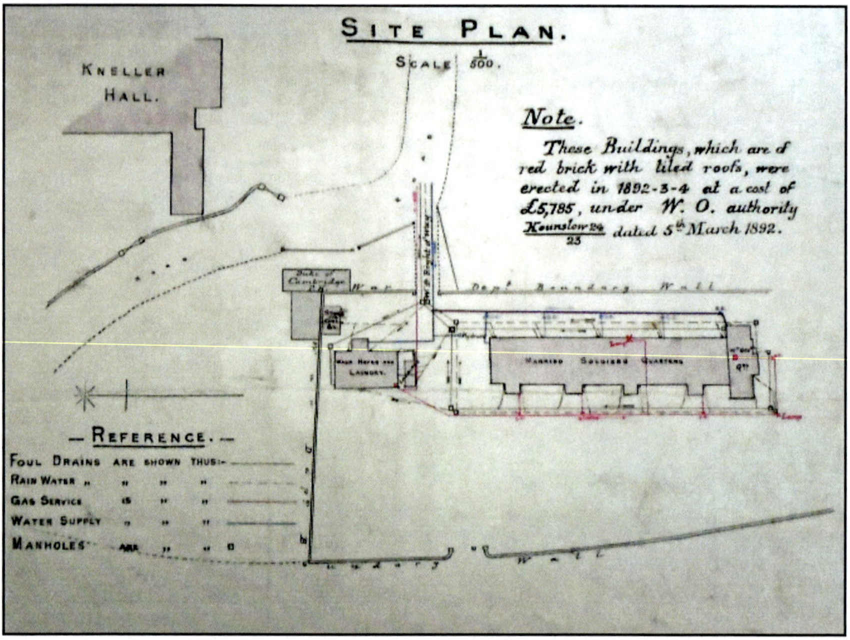

Forming a larger unit at the southern end of the block was the superior Warrant Officer's accommodation comprising a living room, kitchen, scullery and pantry on the ground floor; two bedrooms on the first floor and two attic bedrooms.[39]

The 1901 Census shows an overall increase in the population of Whitton to 1,118, including all military service personnel attached to Kneller Hall. Colonel Francis Bennington-Foote had superseded Colonel Thomas Bradney Shaw-Hillier as the Chief Resident of the School. Adjutant Frederick Henry Mahoney remained the Captain Quartermaster. As second in command, he was joined in the 1891 census by his wife, son and two daughters, and a general domestic servant celebrating in the name of Sarah Squelsh. Ten years later and Kneller Hall accommodated 24 NCOs and 129 Private soldiers, mostly under the age of 19 and each roundly audited as 'Boy.' With days of empire colliding with a poverty-ridden homeland, nine of these boys were born in India and 13 did not know where they were born.

Completing the Hall's complement was William and Harriet Faulkner, Steward and Stewardess respectively. The civilian census enumerator for 1911 picked up a second Lodge within the jurisdiction of the War Department, probably The Croft, where 37-year-old Staff Sergeant Francis Hawkin headed the household. A British subject born in India, Hawkin returned to the mother country sometime before 1887 when he married Chatham girl, Margaret. A year later their first child, William, was born in Southsea, Hampshire. William's younger sister and two brothers were all born in Whitton where the family was posted in 1892. The household was completed with a domestic servant, 17-year-old local girl, Annie Young.

Travel writer H S Vaughn paused on the railway bridge carrying Percy Road through Whitton when there was no station, High Street or the prospect of housing covering the thousands of acres of nursery and arable land. Instead, the bridge presented 'quite a notable view for this part of the world.' Looking eastward was Richmond Hill topped by the Star and Garter hotel. Towards the north-east was Kneller Hall, 'picturesquely rising from the dark woods around Whitton…worthy of Constable's brush – a real piece of old England – stream, meadows and trees.'[40]

The reality, however, was much different. Kneller Hall stood alone as the sole bastion of past times, those dark woods hiding the decay of Whitton Park awaiting a buyer to clear the polluted stream, wild meadows and neglected pastures. Despite a hard-fought battle to save it as a public recreation ground,

Whitton Park was lost, except for its name. Two shopping parades and several new streets of terraced and semi-detached housing had emerged from a short-lived Edwardian building boom. Larger and more desirable semi-detached villas stretched away from Kneller Hall towards Whitton Park, taking advantage of the higher ground, safe from the temperamental brook and distanced from the poverty.

Although Queen Victoria never visited Kneller Hall herself, its summer concerts remained a great attraction to many of her numerous relatives. As part of its Coronation duties in 1902, members of the Royal family were greatly impressed with 'the manner in which the National Anthem was played by the Kneller Hall Band during the Royal progress to and from Westminster.' The eight trumpeters for the Abbey Service was an important milestone in the School's history and musicians from Kneller Hall were prominent at St Paul's Cathedral for the funeral of the (then) longest serving Queen.

In 1906, improvements were made to the chapel at Kneller Hall that provided an opportunity for students to obtain practical experience in the arrangement of church music and Order of Service; a basic requirement of a Bandmaster. New lighting was installed, the oak panelling scraped and cleaned, and the Altar rails replaced. In 1908 a new oak Altar and Reredos was installed, and two windows fitted commemorating past Commandants and Adjutants. A much-needed band practice hall was built that survives behind the Guardroom almost unchanged. And in September 1909, *The Spectator* magazine, reportedly the most influential of all the London Weeklies at this time, added to its diet of politics, culture and current affairs a day's 'netting the lake at Kneller Hall,'[41] offering a unique snapshot of an Edwardian working estate as part of a militarized place of learning.

Such were the improvements made to the lake that it had to be cleared of a healthy stock of fish to create a trout fishery. The Thames Angling Preservation Society undertook the work 'on a sunny August day shaded by noble elms where scores of swallows and martins swept and darted low over the grass, busy among a new hatch of fly.' One pair of swallows provided a confirmed sighting of Repton's boathouse still in situ at the western end of the lake. There was also a dovecot on the island. On the bankside 100 young men and boys dressed in Khaki belonging to many different regiments and with 'two or three negroes among them' carried instruments of every kind, each practicing their own piece before regular practice time. 'They were apparently trying over difficult passages, or repeating favourite airs; no one took any notice of anybody else, but they all played with the utmost abandon and good humour; it was a marvel of flutes, piccolos, trombones, bassoons.'

At nine o'clock the instructors arrived, and the bankside gave way to the fisherman in their high boots and blue jerseys busily unwinding ropes and laying out stretches of netting. Despite a careful search of the lakebed for snags, evidence of the lake's abuse as a local tipping point was manifest in rips and tears to the nets. A cry rang out from the bank as a 10lb carp was landed. The band-music ceased as the students ran to the bankside to witness the landing of four more large fish. Smaller varieties deemed valuable enough for restocking the Thames were placed in a large horse-drawn carrier and driven to the river. The carp had a carrier all to themselves. The day's piscatorial pursuit concluded, the business of training the Army's musicians continued.

The following May those same students quite possibly bore witness to another carriage, one carrying the late King Edward VII to Westminster Hall as part of the greatest assemblage of royalty and rank ever gathered in one place. Some of those same students may have comprised the massed bands under the direction of John Mackenzie Rogan, the legendary senior director of the Brigade of Guards providing the funeral ceremonial. Or perhaps they played a part in the subsequent Coronation of King George V, or as part of the Memorial Service for the 1,635 lives lost in the Titanic disaster held at St Paul's Cathedral on 19 April 1912. Certainly, two years later, all those who trained at Kneller Hall would have been reminded of their days there on reading newspapers reports of the King presenting a pair of swans to grace the lake. 'Nothing could be more suggestive of peace and tranquility,' wrote one observer, blissfully unaware of the unimaginable horror about to visit itself on the world.

1914 – 1947

SOLDIER FIRST STUDENT SECOND

THE PRACTICE OF regiments sending 'uninstructed' and 'weakly' students to Kneller Hall was rife in the early days. Sympathy amongst regiments for the Commandant of the Music School was in short supply almost from the start, fuelled by the belief that a bandsman should be a solider first and musician second. The Commandant of the School of Musketry at Hythe had proposed that bandsmen should be excepted from musketry training, while the Duke of Cambridge felt that it was the first duty of every soldier to master the rifle. With the coming of proficiency pay, a bandsman was required to demonstrate ability in this respect in order to draw a full wage. But once trained, His Royal Highness did not object to bandsmen being relieved from annual training, indicating the first understanding that theirs was a highly specialized function of the Army in its own right. So much so, that on 2 July 1866 the Secretary of State for War, confident that Kneller Hall numbered sufficient armed soldiers, was 'pleased to order the return into the War Office Stores of the arms' that had become surplus to requirements.'[42]

Looking forward 104 years to 1970, it was announced that the 1,612 soldiers of Britain's 52 military bands were all to be trained as medical orderlies in times of general mobilization. Some had already started a three-month course under Army doctors, a move that effectively reversed history from when, following Dunkirk, Winston Churchill ordered medical orderlies into regimental bands to blow a little 'oompah' into the nation's morale.[43] Two decades of peace later and with more money spent on military bands than the arts, service bands were particularly vulnerable to cuts because their end product was perceived as principally morale, which is difficult to quantify let alone equate outside of the special relationship that exists between a band and its regiment. But beyond that is the added value of bandsmen trained as medical orderlies at times of war, a facet brought into sharp focus following the ominous entry in the Royal Military School of Music Historical Record for 4th August 1914:

> 'At 10.30 pm on this date the Order to Mobilise was received and arrangements were at once made to carry out the provisions of the Mobilisation Regulations. All students (except three who belong to the Royal Artillery and Guards) and pupils over 18 years were returned to their units mostly as stretcher-bearers, the role assigned to Bandsmen on mobilization. The resultant vacancies were filled by 13 junior Bandmasters, together with a proportion of their boys and the work of the Establishment continued to be carried out. War declared on Germany at 11pm.'

The band of the Coldstream Guards was playing that night at Whitehall when Captain John Mackenzie Rogan, was informed. He wrote:

> 'There and then I addressed the many thousands gathered round the bandstand and appealed to the young men to enlist and to go forward to fight for their king and country. All joined in singing God Save the King. It was an impressive scene.'

The Royal Military School of Music continued to function at Kneller Hall, although the first afternoon concert of the war years planned for 5 August was cancelled due to rain. Thereafter concerts took place as usual from 15 August and throughout the war years conducted by the retained Bandmasters who dubbed themselves 'the unlucky thirteen,' presumably disappointed not to be joining their regiments in France.[44] However, bands had an important role to play on the Home Front too, performing daily for troops in the London barracks and to the public on Horse Guards Parade, the Royal Parks and Trafalgar Square. The numerous engagements around the country combined these performances with efforts to encourage recruiting. Then the War Office eventually realised the value of bandsmen to boost morale in the ranks and so instruments and music were despatched to France and Belgium, as well the London-based Guards bands on three-month tours. The first was the band of the Grenadier Guards under Captain Albert Williams. Embarking on 22 October 1915 to join the Division at Sailly-Labourse, it earned the distinction of the only Guards band to receive the 1914-15 star.

The Band of the Welsh Guards made its first public appearance on 1 March 1916 when it proceeded to France to meet up with the regiment's 1st Battalion a couple of miles outside Meault just as it was returning from the front line. The battalion was pleasantly surprised to find their regimental band with its Bandmaster, Mr Andrew Harris, waiting at the roadside to play them in as they marched back into the village. During the winter months the band often played in the open during the afternoon at forward areas, as well as Army huts or the town halls in Arras. Against these conditions, the band worked with 'heroic vim and cheerfulness their fingers may have been frozen – their faces were certainly blue – but they played lively tunes without rest.'[45]

On one occasion the Band of the Coldstream Guards met with 'earth-shaking shells exploding all the time a few hundred yards away from us and a big air-fight proceeding simultaneously.' On 11 April 1916 the band was giving a concert in the cinema theatre close to the station at Poperinghe when midway through the building rocked with the ferocity of the fire from German long-range guns. The band finished the performance in record time just before a shell struck the roof of the hall in what turned out to be the worst shelling to date with many killed or wounded. 'The last out of the theatre were the Coldstreamers and the last of the band was Rogan.'[46]

Captain John Mackenzie-Rogan was thought to have been the oldest man serving at The Front, into his 50th year of military service. In his autobiography he recalls the day the band met 3rd battalion Coldstream Guards coming out of the line. 'They, good chaps, were tramping along, each man carrying his seventy or eighty pounds of kit, and many of them bent over with the weight of it. But, at the first tap of the big drum the difference in those self-same men was wonderful to see, and when the band began to play there were cheers you might have heard miles away. It was a wonderous and very affecting experience.'[47] Although regular concerts were given at every opportunity to provide as much music as possible for the men, the courage and bravery displayed by bandsmen in the role of stretcher-bearers, often under heavy fire, cannot be overemphasized.

Such valour was recognised with the award of well over 100 medals for gallantry, including the Victoria Cross awarded to Thomas Edward Rendle, a

29-year-old bandsman in the 1st Battalion, The Duke of Cornwall Light Infantry who attended many wounded under heavy rifle and shell fire. Phase Two training at Kneller Hall is known as Rendle VC Troop in his honour. The first recorded casualty was Lt Colonel B E Ward, 1st Battalion Middlesex Regiment who died of his wounds 26 October 1914[48] and as to the class of that year, Gordon and Alwyn Turner in their book *The Trumpets Will Sound* include a list of 15 students who graduated that year, although, at the time of writing, it has only been possible to trace one of them and that is George Albert Cunningham Herniman.[49]

A Londoner born in 1881, George Herniman was ten years later an inmate at the Upper Edmonton Union Workhouse School. He joined the army around 1895 aged 14; married Glaswegian Mary Crighton Brown in 1906 and is listed in the 1911 census as a Military Musician in the Irish Guards. In 1914 he was a bandsman at Kneller Hall occupying the Married Quarters as Warrant Officer Class 1 in the 2nd Battalion Devonshire Regiment. Having taken part in the 1914 Christmas Truce, the Battalion saw action across the Western Front up until the final advance in Artois on 11 November 1918, by which time George's active service was at an end. The Bandmaster Lists for 1916 – 1922 have him living in Devon in 1917 where he is recorded as a

Bandmaster W.O (Warrant Officer). By 1932 he was at the Gordon Boys' Home in Chobham, Surrey, where he retired as a Pensioner Bandmaster in 1946. In 1956, aged 75, he was living in Isleworth and died in Middlesbrough, aged 84, in 1966.

In a cruel irony as the war drew to its conclusion are the graves of three bandmasters laid to rest in Twickenham Cemetery who died between September and November 1918. Not as a result of combat along with the 64 other fallen servicemen in the same cemetery, but a second wave of global death that decimated a fifth of the world's population. Bandmaster R W Ramsey of 2nd Battalion Royal Inniskilling Fusiliers died 26 September 1918; J J Burkmann: 38920, 3rd Battalion Somerset Light Infantry died 3 November that same year and 31-year-old T Rowbotham, 3rd Battalion Irish Guards died 20 days later.[50] Manchester born Thomas Rowbotham lived locally in Twickenham where he married Kate Dixon at Holy Trinity Church on 25 January 1915. When he died he was living in Staten Gardens, a mile or so from Kneller Hall. No cause of death is given for the three bandsmen, but the timing is hugely significant.

A 20-year-old nurse named Phyliss Burn was also buried in Twickenham Cemetery in November 1918. She came to prominence in 2002 when a group of scientists were looking to learn more about the lethal influenza virus between May 1918 and December 1920.[51] They found her grave after scouring death registers throughout the country for information on flu victims whose remains were likely to be in good condition because they were buried in lead coffins. The research team from St Bartholomew's Hospital in London traced relatives for permission to exhume the body of Phylis 'Hillie' Burn who contracted the lethal virus as a volunteer nurse. She lies alongside her father, James Montague Burn, a major in the Royal Engineers in India and South Africa. Her mother and two younger sisters are believed not to have attended Phyllis' funeral because she knew her fate when she contracted the infection in October 1918 and decided to die alone to protect her family.

The Annual Report of the Medical Officer of Health for Twickenham for 1918 contained the grim realization that the epidemics of influenza, first identified in July and towards the close of the year 'produced an effect on public health which has not been equalled in seriousness by any epidemic outbreak in our time.'[52] The three bandmasters and nurse Burn were brought down during the second period of the pandemic. There was no effective means of preventing the spread of infection. The severe character of the illness often transmuted to pneumonia, rendering what little medical treatment there was all but futile. The difficulties dealing with the enormous number of cases in October and November was exacerbated by the lack of doctors on military service and no hospital beds (military or civilian).

From 1919 no other casualties of the flu pandemic are known to have affected the business of Kneller Hall as the School resumed business. With visits by composers such as Sir Henry Wood, Gustav Holst and Vaughn Williams conducting their own works, there was still much to be done to bring Army music into line with the International, or Continental pitch adopted by the Philharmonic as far back as 1885.[53] Improvements to the physical structure of Kneller Hall included converting the former Students' Mess into the Guardroom. In January 1920 the ornamental lake was emptied and cleaned. A year later a new bandstand was constructed and in the spring of 1924, the first of 20 or so sound-proof lecture rooms and Professors' individual teaching rooms were constructed, followed by the installation of electric lighting throughout the School. Externally, massed military band displays at great national events became an increasing feature, such as at the British Empire Exhibition. Hardly a week went by in the summer months where a regimental band wasn't engaged in one public event or another.

It was therefore inevitable that the world of commercial engagement would encroach on the military's public service remit to train musicians for military and ceremonial duties. The only exception to this had been a series of Sunday concerts at the Alhambra theatre in London, then enjoying the last days of variety. These concerts were organised by the Sunday League that looked to 'promote interesting and elevating recreation' on the Lord's Day and were licensed by the London County Council for band, orchestra and song, but no acting. Out of this it was decided to form a commercial arm of the school with the Kneller Hall No.1 Band at its core. With a projected income upwards of £6,000 a year reducing costs to the public purse, there was little by way of objection to what is nowadays a familiar concept. As well as a full programme of summer season engagements around the country, there was a booking at the Ranelagh Polo Club every Saturday, Sunday and Wednesday, and the band's first appearance on the BBC, first broadcasting from Savoy Hill 8 July 1924.

In 1926, the War Department decided to sell Kneller Hall's North Field, described by the land agent as 'a valuable area of parkland situated between Twickenham and Hounslow stations...close to a bus route and the International Rugby Football Ground.'[54] Despite the 14 acres providing an excellent opportunity at a time when land fringing the capital was ripe for building development, open to an offer for a quick sale, it was eventually sold for £3,000. Meanwhile, a nine-hole golf course was laid out on the Sports Field to the south and the wooden bandstand replaced with a semi-circular reinforced concrete stage that became known as The Rock. This enjoyed excellent acoustic properties and was able to accommodate 160 musicians. It lasted until 1995, considerably longer than its replacement already showing serious signs of deterioration. By 1935 the North Field had made way for the suburban ideal with the Whitton Tennis Club together with allotments (giving way to Amberside Close in the 1980s) creating a substantial barrier between War Department land and the Kneller Gardens Housing Estate.

Elsewhere in Whitton gaps left by Edwardian speculative builders who failed to satisfy lower middle-class aspirations were plugged with homes for the working classes and returned war heroes. As the 1930s Great Depression hit hard other pockets of the country, so London enjoyed a boom period in the growth of a new phenomenon for the working and lower middle classes known as home ownership. Most still had jobs and with low prices and interest rates, money with which to buy a house was very cheap to borrow. The last remnants of Whitton Park were relentlessly being cleared as construction of the Great Chertsey Road opened-up the district to the capital for the first time. Complete with its own railway station and purpose-built High Street, within eight years virtually all open land surrounding Kneller Hall was buried beneath a tide of bricks and mortar. In 1933, Warren Road bypassed the circuitous medieval route fronting the School of Military Music estate. The Commandant was unhappy with the resultant inconveniences, complaining to Twickenham council about a fair held on the open ground fronting the mansion. In reply, Twickenham council reported that the fair would be gone when the land was required for building, which was imminent.[55]

The commandant further complained about one new housing development taking the name 'Kneller Hall Estate,' which he claimed should remain limited to the War Office property alone. Again, the local authority was unable to offer a reassuring view.[56] The days of splendid isolation were over. With new neighbours at every turn, a real sense of unease is detected in further correspondence with the local authorities. The War Department's detailed proposals for development after moving the Royal Military School of Music to Canterbury created a chorus of dismay from the Twickenham Ratepayers Association, which called upon Twickenham Borough to make immediate representations to the War Office. Echoing precisely the same outrage expressed 50 and 70 years later, the local community viewed the threat 'with very great alarm as a disaster for Twickenham and surrounding areas.' It called upon the support of the local Member of Parliament to preserve the presence of the School as being 'of great benefit to the borough and its removal would probably mean the disappearance of yet another badly needed open space.'[57]

Whitehall had other ideas. The defence budget was under particular attack. A committee, including the Commandant of Kneller Hall, visited the proposed Canterbury relocation and agreed it could be made suitable with the provision of a practice room, a bandstand, silent rooms and central heating. But then there was the problem of the visiting professors, most of whom lived and worked in London. Canterbury was simply too far for them to commute on a regular basis and without them the reputation of the School would suffer significantly. The proposed move to Canterbury was therefore dropped on 5 April 1934.

Two years later and local council business included in the Provision for Kneller Hall the widening of Kneller Road to 50 feet and Whitton Dene to 40 feet.[58] The purpose was clear to the Twickenham Ratepayers Association with regard to compliance with the Town Planning Scheme as a residential area as opposed to a private or public open space should the War Office's intimations of Kneller Hall becoming surplus to military requirements. In such a case an offer would be made to the local authority to buy the estate before going onto the open market. However, as the 1930s drew to a close, a more pressing matter focused attention elsewhere.

Although war was declared with Nazi Germany on 1 September 1939, the British government had been preparing for the expectation of bombing raids on civilian targets for three years. The Air Raid Wardens Service was set up in 1937 aimed at reporting incidents, reassuring the public and providing Air Raid Precautions (ARP) advice as to how to extinguish small fires, administer first aid and investigate reports of unexploded bombs. The Women's Voluntary Service (WVS) was set up in 1938 when gas-masks were issued, the first domestic air-raid shelters were distributed, and public shelters built. By 1939, a comprehensive set of plans for communal and public shelters across Twickenham Borough had been drawn up.[59]

One of the first significant considerations of the effects of air raids in preparation for war was made in 1936 with the proposed evacuation of government staff from Whitehall. The list of criteria drawn up included finding suitable domestic and office accommodation in places relatively safe from air attack and with adequate communications facilities. Minimal preparation was a prerequisite and with public knowledge kept to a minimum. In this, Kneller Hall, 10 miles west of Whitehall was a prime candidate and immediately following the outbreak of war, officers and staff under Sir Walter Kirke, Commander-in-Chief Home Forces, moved in to establish the General Headquarters for the defence of Britain against invasion.

Although local authorities were instructed to survey all potential basement accommodation, there's no evidence that Twickenham Borough did so to any great extent, despite there being very competent Borough Engineers with the knowledge of how far structures of varying age and types would permit safe reinforcement. A public shelter for 180 people was constructed in the grounds of York House, the administrative centre for the borough, but with no evidence of fortification to the mansion's 17th century cellars. Nor was the underground warren at Kneller Hall reinforced, although the wooden slatted ceilings are in parts punctuated by distinctly 20th century steel lintels. Faded blue directions stenciled on the walls point to various 19th century brick-lined chambers with their heavy metal doors making for ready shelters. At the heart of this former high-Victorian servant domain, and best protected, is the Operations Room still available to organise, evaluate and provide an ordered information flow as required.

Regimental Bands ceased to exist when the mobilisation order was issued on 28 September 1939. In between filling sandbags and performing guard duties, the 30 junior music students remaining continued their studies until 5 December when a convoy of lorries transferred them and remaining music school staff to Churchill House, Aldershot. The shifting of the many thousands of music journals was a major task in itself. The School Commandant, Colonel J A A Griffin had already left to take up an active service appointment, leaving Major Adkins in command as well as Director of Music. Together with the School Regimental Sergeant Major and one cook, senior student G H Stunnell, recently qualified as Bandmaster, was appointed Professor of Theory. As well as postal tuition and the students themselves helping teach one another, the school continued to function.

Within a few weeks of the German invasion of Poland, practically all of the trained and properly equipped troops in the United Kingdom sailed for

France, leaving the country woefully short of much in the way of a credible ground defence. General Kirke was an experienced soldier in the field who had served as Inspector-General of the Territorial Army and Inspector-General of Home Defence since May 1939. As Commander-in-Chief, Home Forces, he was responsible for the five major UK commands. With limited powers continually frustrated by the War Office, he moved his General Headquarters at Horse Guards in Whitehall to Kneller Hall on 7 September 1939 where he formulated the principles of his 'Julius Caesar Plan' that centered on the premise the enemy would try to capture an East Coast port to enable the landing of heavy stores to promote an all-out invasion.[60]

However, the rapid pace of events soon rendered his plan obsolete and set in motion a drastic revision. On 16 May 1940, the Allied armies in Belgium began their long withdrawal against a mighty German onslaught, leading to the surrender of the Belgium army leaving British and French forces trapped around Dunkirk. Back home, a coalition had been formed under Winston Churchill, heralding a more dynamic attitude to the conduct of the war in general and the question of invasion in particular. Churchill had set up the Defence Committee, headed by himself as Minister of Defence, while the Chiefs of Staff formed the Home Defence Executive to supervise the drastic overhaul of measures for defence, which granted General Kirke more control over the military and a greater influence on Civil Defence. But with such a meagre and inadequate collection of a mostly semi-trained and poorly resourced home guard, Kirke's days were numbered.

Waiting in the wings was the Chief of the Imperial General Staff, General Ironside, who had gained the confidence of the Cabinet. Kirke met his successor at Kneller Hall on 27 May 1940 where Ironside took up his post, less than impressed with what he described as a 'most awful Victorian country-house,' but where a 'comfortable little mess' had been made up.[61] Surrounded by green grass it was all very different from London. Although his installation there was to be short-lived, the effect on the whole of the British landscape was as immediate as it was profound. Given the size of his forces and their lack of equipment, Ironside pushed for the creation of a network of internal fortifications in the form of pillboxes, tank traps and other barricades that still punctuate the country to this day. While the detailed layout of these barriers evolved over June and July 1940, the Ironside Plan replacing Kirke's Julius Caesar Plan began immediately.[62]

Ironside, however, provoked intense debate and controversy with his own plan that made little mention of defending the South Coast. Deemed by the Chiefs of Staff to be completely unsound, Vice Chief of the Imperial General Staff, General John Dill, called an emergency meeting with Ironside at Kneller Hall to discuss his Operational Instructions for the Defence of the Country. Despite the worries of the Vice-Chiefs centring on a renewed spate of invasion rumours, Ironside busied himself with a move of his headquarters from Kneller Hall to St. Paul's School in Hammersmith.[63] Less than 10 minutes from Whitehall, he argued he would be better able to conduct the fight in person in a proper Combined Operations Room than the limited space of the Cabinet War Room where he was likely to be continually called away for conferences and meetings. His assertion that contact between him and the Government could be maintained perfectly well by telephone and liaison officers was not met with enthusiasm by Winston Churchill who replaced him with Lt.-Gen. Sir Alan Brooke.

Ironside's legacy at Kneller Hall continued for a brief period in the form of a Special Forces unit set up to assist the Royal Corps of Signals in the constant battle to progress communications from the front line to Headquarters. Initially taking the name the 'Ironsiders,' the unit took on the more formal designation No 1 General Headquarters (GHQ) Reconnaissance Unit, which changed to the Reconnaissance Corps before settling on GHQ Liaison Regiment, or as it became known, Phantom. Under the direct command of GHQ, Home Forces, the new regiment initially consisted of an HQ at Kneller Hall and three scout car groups but expanded swiftly moving out to Richmond Park with 48 officers, 407 other ranks and a pigeon loft with 500 birds.[64]

No more is known about what went on at Kneller Hall between late 1940 and March 1945. In common with hundreds of other private schools and stately homes throughout the country, Kneller Hall may have served as a training centre, or 'X' Station, used by the Special Operations Executive (SOE). The list for these stations is incomplete. When radio stations were separated from Bletchley Park (Station X) in June 1942, each station was given a Roman numeral code number, many of which are unknown. Kneller Hall and its grounds wouldn't have been suitable for combat training involving weapons or explosives but could have served as a Senior Officers School or Students Assessment Board. It may have been involved with experimental work, even storage or production. The Natural History Museum's Demonstration Room, for example, came under the Camouflage Section as a training centre for agents and for briefing officials. For sure, Kneller Hall could not have sat out the entire war empty and abandoned.

Twickenham Borough as a whole had devolved down the local headquarters of its own offices, its officers and key representatives across a huge variety of responsibilities and locations. Park pavilions became ARP stations and rest centres; an Auxiliary Fire Station occupied one uncompleted store in Whitton High Street opposite another recent addition that became a Civic restaurant offering one hot meal a day to bombed-out civilians. Twickenham's famous rugby ground housed ambulances under its vast sheds converted into coal yards; its restaurants and bars given over to rest and decontamination centres. Even its hallowed turf was used for grazing, unlike the 10 or so acres next door at Kneller Hall, which make no appearance in the Borough's comprehensive *Notes on Invasion Defence*, a weighty tome stamped 'Very Secret' that describes in detail the various strategic positions within 10 District sub-divisions.[65]

District 1 defined Whitton south of the railway line, or what we know today as Heathfield and was codenamed Andrew. Whitton north of the line comprised District 2. Codenamed Arthur this area included Kneller Hall, although no mention is made of it. Districts Andrew and Arthur joined with David (East Twickenham) north of an anti-tank line expressed by the railway. If the seven other Districts south of that line fell, then administration would have fallen to the Invasion Defence Officer for neighbouring Heston and Isleworth. Whitton suffered random attacks or collateral damage from attempts to bomb the Feltham marshalling yards. The worst damage occurred during the Blitz from the autumn and winter of 1940 to March 1941. In 1944 a V1 flying bomb hit the High Street killing several people and destroying or damaging 60 shops. In total, 46 houses close to Kneller Hall were destroyed during the war and a further 232 badly damaged.[66]

Thanks to the amateur reporting of one remarkably well-informed local bomb-spotter, we know that one high explosive device landed in the grounds of Kneller Hall during the heavy raids of 29th and 30th November 1940, but with no damage to the house.[67] At the start of the year, the students transferred to Aldershot escaped unharmed after a bomb exploded 50 yards from the front of Churchill House. This incident, which took place on the night of 9/10 January 1941, represents the single reference to the Army School of Music in the Kneller Hall historical record.

By 1944, Churchill particularly had realised the loss of Regimental Bands as a means of maintaining morale and decided they should be re-formed, although some Units had already succeeded in raising unofficial Bands. One telling example of the importance of Regimental Bands at times of conflict comes by way of a battalion of Irish Guards making its way north through Italy bound for Anzio. On a cheerless New Year's evening in 1944 the cold and wet was vanquished by a visit from the Regimental Band touring the Mediterranean in 3-ton lorries. An observer wrote in his diary of Captain Willcocks who led his 30-strong band ahead of the Battalion to the Regimental March 'St Patrick's Day' and other rousing tunes. Italians lined the pavements clapping and cheering. 'It was the way men should go to war.'[68]

Major Willcocks, as he became, was a classic product of Kneller Hall, having transferred from the workhouse to become a boy cornetist with the 4th

Battalion Royal Fusiliers in 1915 and in 1924 one of four students who subsequently reached the top of their profession. Having obtained his Bandmaster diploma, he conducted the Band of the 2nd battalion South Wales Borderers before becoming Bandmaster of the Royal Artillery in 1937. A year later he joined the Irish Guards where he eventually achieved the rank of Major and became Director of Music. Going on to enjoy celebrity status in peacetime, at his funeral in 1962 the pipes of the Irish Guards regimental band were joined by a fanfare of the Kneller Hall trumpeters.

In March 1945, the War Office began establishing Civil Resettlement Units (CRU) to receive the first wave of Prisoners of War returning from Germany.[69] Hatfield House became CRU Headquarters. Other country houses across Britain, including Kneller Hall, were adapted for use so that men could attend close to where they lived. Each unit had a Commanding Officer, a Second-in-Command, a Medical Officer (usually a psychiatrist), a Vocational Officer, Ministry of Labour Liaison and a Civil Liaison Officer, usually a woman trained in psychological methods. POWs especially might not have interacted with women for years, so female staff were intended to help repatriates become more comfortable in mixed company.

All attendees to these centres were volunteers, arriving in four batches of 15 per week. Following introductory talks from the Commanding Officer and the Medical Officer there was an interview after which participants were left to attend workshops, visit nearby workplaces or have work-experience placements. They were able to attend group discussions, meet with the Vocational Officer to talk about careers and with the Civil Liaison Officer to talk about social or relationship concerns. Whist Drives and dances were held, inviting the local civilian population to assist in the repatriation process. Men were not required to wear their military uniforms except for the pay parade when they were given their salaries.

Just before the Kneller Hall centre opened in May 1945, a letter was received by Twickenham Council from the Sports Officer, 668 Artisan Works Company, Royal Engineers, newly moved into the area and keen to apply for the use of a cricket pitch and nets in the borough. In another unrelated letter to the Council, Eastern Command and the London District Land Agent jointly urged Twickenham's Medical Officer to liaise with the War Department to clear the stagnant lake at Kneller Hall. In a rare moment of joined-up government, Twickenham Council suggested 668 Artisan Works Company consider the sporting facilities at Kneller Hall in return for their particular skills in remedying the situation.[70] 668 Artisan Works were probably responsible for the building of a circle of concrete Nissen Huts on the playing field. Complete with a central wash-house, this commune was supposed to provide temporary accommodation and workshops for attendee repatriates but survived as classrooms and student billets until 1957 when new accommodation blocks were built.

A Pathe Newsreel for 1946, entitled *Britain Mends Men for Industry*, earnestly posed the question what happened to returning servicemen? 'We didn't know,' admits the narrator brightly, 'but here at Kneller Hall, Twickenham, we intend to find out!' The brief report informs us that there

1947 RAF aerial photograph showing the resettlement complex fanned out in a series of Nissen huts laid due east of the mansion. Also, the tree-lined extent of the ornamental lake running the entire length of the northern boundary.

were never less than 250 ex-servicemen at Kneller Hall, some officers, some rankers, some fit, some disabled. Most of them were ex-prisoners of war facing up to the tough job of getting back into civilian life. They lived as they liked and did whatever work they chose to do. It was an experiment, but it got results. Signing off, the narrator exclaims 'and that's Kneller Hall, the Army's leading resettlement centre!' A sister newsreel entitled *Army Resettlement Unit* has no soundtrack, only images of former soldiers strolling around the grounds, busy in workshops, drinking tea and playing tennis.

1947 – 2016

A Little More Oompah

The Royal Military School of Music resumed normal business on 1 November 1946 after a seven-year absence. By the end of March 1947, all returned POWs and ex-servicemen attending Kneller Hall had left to begin new lives elsewhere. One hundred and ten student bandsmen assembled to form the initial post-war pupils' course, performing the first concert on 7 May 1948 to an audience of just 445, a figure which, by the final performance of the season on 24 September, had grown to an estimated attendance of 26,000. Two years later the total seasonal audience had risen to more than 34,000. That the Army was here to stay was underlined by a planning application submitted to Twickenham Borough for a large chunk of the Sports Field along Kneller Road currently taken up with allotments to build 80 residential flats and garages for married officers.[71]

The local community and council members were not impressed, arguing this would spoil a rare expanse of open ground that had 'from time immemorial formed an attractive open space.' The matter was brought to the Middlesex Country Council to join with Twickenham Corporation in discussions with the War Department. On 16 November 1949, a conference was held by County Planning where the War Department reported it had been unable to find an alternative site for this badly-needed accommodation even as far as Hounslow Heath. The Treasury had no money to assist and the mood of the conference was to retain the open ground as part of the Greater London Plan.[72]

On 3 February 1950, the Town Clerk reported that the Minister of Town and Country Planning appreciated the desire to retain an open space especially where they were deficient as in Whitton, but also understood the War Department's need for housing and the lack of alternative sites. Because of the particular difficulties for the military, the Minister regretfully found in favour of the War Department. Whilst recognising this decision would be disappointing, he hoped for full co-operation in securing the development. And so it transpired, for in considering the wider context within a local plan to build a new primary school, a new arrangement emerged embracing both needs and resulting in the built and open landscape as it appears today.[73]

The eastern boundary of the Kneller Hall estate towards the Duke's river was to say the least, irregular. A new school was proposed along the boundary within a very modest 70 feet niche between the river and War Department land currently used as allotments. The new plan looked to increase the school's footprint considerably to 315 feet; protect the trees close to the river bank and straighten up the irregular 'Cut Throat Alley'[74] which poorly represented the War Department's eastern boundary. A less convoluted footpath would run adjacent to a new road servicing an amended alignment of flats running north-south instead of east west across the face of the open ground. With no objections received regarding the height of the proposed development in view of the proximity to the rugby ground stands, the plans were approved to provide for both the Duke of Cambridge Close and Chase Bridge school.[75]

The first weekly concert from Kneller Hall was televised on 19 July 1950. A year later and the newly-formed Band of the Women's Royal Army Corps

(WRAC) made its first appearance as part of a grand concert at the Albert Hall featuring over 300 performers. In 1953, the first woman student, Captain J B MacDowal of the WRAC, entered Kneller Hall, going on to enjoy a particularly successful course that eventually saw her appointed Director of Music, WRAC Regimental Band. Her Majesty the Queen inspected pupils and students on parade at Kneller Hall on 28 June 1957 and toured the school, pausing to unveil a plaque commemorating its founding a century earlier by H.R.H. The Duke of Cambridge.

It has been said the 1950s were in black and white and the sixties were in Technicolor. To many, the so-called Swinging Sixties remain the defining decade of post-war Britain. London led the world in fashion and ground-breaking music. Together with the news spiced with a scandalous mix of sex and spies came the first James Bond movie and the contraceptive pill. As Eel Pie Island was fast becoming the epicentre of an emerging Rhythm n' Blues music scene, so a mile north filming for the epic 1962 feature film Lawrence of Arabia was swapping Spain, Jordan, Morocco and the deserts of the United States for the home of military music.

For many of the film's Middle Eastern settings, director David Lean used the heavily Moorish city of Seville. The 'Cairo' officers' club was where Lawrence's Arab companion is refused a drink after the desert crossing. As a last-minute stand-in for the arcaded building used as the club, truckloads of sand were brought in to cover Kneller Hall's parade ground giving it a more exotic appearance. A band comprising 60 students and pupils was assembled in period uniforms to the musical direction of Basil Brown and the Band Sgt Major Trevor Sharpe, 'a brilliant composer of military music.' The film company

listened to eight marches and chose Alford's Voice of the Gods. The eventual fee of £8 7s 6d per musician was a small fortune to the performers who waited five days for the sun to shine.[76]

Twickenham as a Borough ceased to exist in 1965 with the creation of Greater London as part of a new local government structure for the capital significantly reducing the number of local authorities responsible for larger areas and populations. The London Borough of Richmond-upon-Thames was the name given by government for the amalgamation of Twickenham with Richmond, Kew, Barnes and Mortlake. Owned and administered by the newly-formed Ministry of Defence, Kneller Hall continued unaffected by all of this apart from abiding by national and local planning and regulatory requirements. Consent was required of the new London Borough of Richmond-upon-Thames in 1967 to build a concert hall in the grounds of Kneller Hall. At a cost of £50,000 it was designed to provide for indoor performances during the winter months, thus boosting income. The first series of winter concerts was staged there from 18 December 1967 to March the following year featuring performances by the four separate company bands, each comprising 60 players.[77]

Some of the 1,612 soldiers in Britain's regimental bands had already trained as medical orderlies to double up in times of general mobilisation. Some had already started a three-month course under the supervision of Army doctors with a two-week refresher each subsequent year. Writing about this in *The Times*, Henry Stanhope claimed that 25 years after Winston Churchill's call for medical orderlies to 'blow a little oompah' into the equation, there was even more need with the General Army Reserve having replaced National Service when it ended in 1963. Such a move would provide added protection for the bands when the Treasury came looking for more defence cuts at a time when more was being spent on military bands than on the Arts. The 1970s were desperately difficult politically and economically with endless strikes and a three-day week. The sum of £7m quoted by critics, however, included the cost of clothing, housing and food for troops in all the regimental bands who also performed normal soldiering duties. 'But predators at the time seemed to be hovering over every euphonium,' Stanhope reported.[78]

He predicted that by the end of 1972, the number of Army bands would have been reduced from 92 to 75, comprising 52 regimental bands with 31 players; 10 minor staff bands of 31; two household cavalry bands with 44 players in each; nine major staff bands including the foot guards with 55 players; the band of the Royal Artillery with an 85-strong band and the band of the Gurkhas. The RAF's nine bands, including the Women's Royal Air Force and the 15 Royal Marines bands that also served the Royal Navy, would be reduced to nine bands after 1972. The thinking behind this lay in the perception that while morale is principally the end product of services' bands where a rousing rendition of The British Grenadiers may augment a state occasion, it no longer has a place alongside troops engaged in a fire fight.

Notwithstanding, Kneller Hall remained the mecca of Army bandsmen. Only the best attended there. And there was ambition. Not every bandsman wanted to play with the Guards, as promotion there was too slow. The goal for some was to move from band to band earning promotion each time, with the ultimate target of becoming a Director of Music. Twenty years before it would become a reality, one of the greatest fears amongst these aspiring musicians was the unification of all bands into a single military service from where they could be posted to a unit as and when required. As it stood, most military musicians cherished the special relationship they enjoyed with the regiment they had chosen to join.

A new practice room was built in 1972 attaching the Concert Hall to be named after Brigadier Charles Morris, a former Commandant of Kneller Hall. Lasting barely a fortnight, today only its footprint remains as a slab of tarmac east of the Mansion and before the sports field. Workmen were re-felting the Concert Hall roof when it caved in on some 150 bandsmen rehearsing for a charity concert. The *Daily Telegraph* reported: 'the bandsmen dropped their instruments and ran for

cover as tons of masonry came crashing from the roof.'[79] However, photos in the local newspaper show a much less robust-looking construction of thin plywood and slender timber beams.[80] The subsequent collapse of thinly-fabricated brick retaining walls demonstrate how much of a danger this building represented to the public as well as Army bandsmen.

Having survived potentially a much greater disaster, the School was left to provide a temporary indoor concert venue, which took the form of an inflatable dome costing £7,000 that couldn't be inflated in times of high winds. Planning permission requirements were mildly addressed in the choosing of a green-coloured dome designed to blend in with the grass of the sports field. Worst of all were the acoustics, with one wag suggesting that the best result was to have the band inside the dome and the audience outside, which defeated the whole object of the exercise.[81] The inadequacy of the structure was amply demonstrated across each winter season where the rocket-like heating engines burned all day to inadequately raise the temperature of the interior.

Meanwhile, the 'Troubles' of Northern Ireland were being played out on the streets of the British mainland. In retaliation for the shootings by British soldiers in Derry, known as Bloody Sunday, Official IRA volunteers drove a car laden with explosives into an unsecured army base in Aldershot. The ‘mainland campaign’, as it became known, looked to increase public and media pressure on the British government. The military was a prime target. In February 1974, a coach carrying soldiers and their families in northern England was bombed by the IRA killing 12 people and injuring 14. In July 1982 eight soldiers on ceremonial duty were killed in two IRA bomb blasts in Hyde Park and Regents Park. In September 1989 a bomb at the Royal Marines Music School in Deal killed 11 and wounded 22. An explosion at an Army recruitment centre in Leicester in February 1990 wounded two and in May seven were wounded at an Army Educational Service Headquarters in Eltham. One soldier was killed by a car bomb in Wembley and in June, another was shot dead at a train station in Litchfield.

Throughout this long and bloody period there were no known attacks planned or made on Kneller Hall. For obvious reasons the national and local news services didn’t highlight such very real possibilities. While service uniform was no longer a familiar sight on the streets of Whitton where local pubs, shops and businesses became potential targets, the band still played on at the annual carnival, Christmas Parade and other traditional local performances. Within and without the School a new compound emerged less insecure. The traditional multifarious mixture of iron railings, concrete paneling and chain fencing was largely replaced with razor wire, closed-circuit TV and armed soldiers openly patrolling the grounds and marshalling the summer concerts.

Mercifully, the most serious matter vexing Kneller Hall was controversy surrounding the shifting of the summer concerts from Wednesday to Thursday evenings so as not to clash with the BBC’s hugely successful *Sportsnight* programme found to be decimating audiences.[82] In the 1981 edition of the Kneller Hall magazine *Fanfare*, the Commandant, Colonel Tim Beath, reflected on the long-overdue departure of the indoor concert dome:

> ‘After eight years of valiant but barely satisfactory service, this vast, panting, hippopotamus-like creature, increasingly held together by masking tape and with an ailing heart (or engine) has finally been borne away. The trouble is that its demise has not coincided with the birth of our new Concert Hall. The cold eye of the Financier lit upon the plans and in the present straightened circumstances that was that

> – for the time being. We live in the hope that this essential new facility will soon be given the go-ahead, but for the present the facilities of the Home of Military Music are slim indeed; we need even to apply for authority to use the former RSMs Quarter practice rooms.'[83]

The Kneller Hall trumpeters and percussionists played as part of the Military Music Pageant at Wembley in the presence of Prince Charles and Lady Diana Spencer, with the trumpeters again invited to play for the royal wedding in July. The following day a celebratory summer concert at Kneller Hall attracted an audience of 6,000 but was overshadowed by the question of government spending on Defence. As part of wider moves to combat the 1983 recession a comprehensive survey of Kneller Hall was undertaken that confirmed the poor condition of the mansion, the spartan and insufficient student accommodation and a bill of £1.6m to fix it. It's possible that part of the costs were covered by the sale of the characterful Victorian Married Quarters now given way to the less distinctive dwellings occupying the old walled garden, although it has not been possible to confirm this.

A decision was taken to cut staffing levels by 550, leaving an overall establishment of 2,000 army musicians, just as Henry Stanhope had predicted in his Times article a decade earlier. But that was only the start. As well as senior posts responsible for managing, supervising and recruiting musicians being replaced with just two directorial posts, the 1934 proposal to vacate Kneller Hall returned to the political agenda in the form of a merger of the three services music schools.

This restructuring was criticized by several British politicians, but in particular the late Toby Jessel, Member of Parliament for Twickenham, who took to the floor numerous times in response the MOD's Front Line First case study that recognised no sacred cows in the examination of support activities.[84] The Royal Marine Band's base at Deal was mooted as the likely future location for a tri-service school of music. It had taken a more radical approach to training within civilian schools through bursaries. Here it was argued, would be preserved the excellent standards of service musicians in a more cost-effective way and with no basic training school of music needed anywhere by the turn of the century.

Bringing the issue of cost-effectiveness into sharper focus was the suggestion that existing buildings at HMS Nelson in Portsmouth could be adapted into a musical training facility for less than a month's worth of the overall annual running cost of Deal. Here, it was argued, immediate, significant and sensible economies could be achieved by locating a school of military music at the centre of an existing naval concentration. In response, Toby Jessel called on the House to protest and to encourage support for the plans to be scrapped. He made it plain that 'without doubt we need to retain a military school of music whether on its own or merged with the training of Royal Marine bands which would, of course, be warmly welcomed at Twickenham if, unfortunately, they were not able to stay at Deal.'

The Member for Dover, David Shaw, interjected: 'Does my Honourable Friend accept that if there were to be combined school of music his bandsmen would also be welcome at Deal?' To which Jessel replied, 'I am sure that they would be welcome, but they would not be welcome to leave Twickenham.'

Jessel argued that Kneller Hall was world-renowned. A large sum of money had recently been spent on its renovation. It was the largest of the three British military music schools and the closest to central London to draw on top-class specialist music tuition and large audiences. In support, the Member for Brentford and Isleworth Mr. Nirj Joseph Deva added that Kneller Hall represented a very important attribute to the welfare and cultural aspects of his constituents, particularly the deprived parts of his constituency who had only Kneller Hall to go to for some form of cultural activity.

Toby Jessel hoped that the Minister would confirm that the Government would never countenance any suggestion that army bandsmen should be trained at civilian music colleges. Although second to none in his admiration of the country's symphony orchestras, these colleges were not equipped to train military musicians to march as they played and to stay exactly in line with military precision out of doors and in all weathers. He won the day and the Royal Marines School of Music at Deal was chosen to close in April 1996.

David Shaw called it a disaster and a disgrace, claiming that the 42-acre site had not been given the attention it should have been over the years. Had the proposals put forward back in the 1980s been adopted then Deal had the capacity to take on a new lease of life as the centre of a combined defence school of music.

Shaw argued that the bandsmen trained in Deal were commonly regarded as probably the best in the world as much as those trained at Kneller Hall and RAF Uxbridge. Despite its costing £72,000 a man per year to train a student at Deal, as against £16,000 to train a bandsman at Kneller Hall, he paid scornful tribute to the Members for Twickenham and Brentford and Isleworth in managing to keep Kneller Hall open for so long despite the aircraft noise interfering with music practice and public concerts, and the lack of practice rooms for the students, only their bedrooms. Deal boasted wonderful facilities. Also, the property value of Kneller Hall was upwards of £15 million and of enormous benefit to taxpayers.

The late Toby Jessel MP conducting at Kneller Hall in 1996.

Throughout this intense political and public discourse, the Secretary of State for Defence (Michael Heseltine) favoured Edinburgh as a site for the Army bands as another means of devolving government money and resources around the country. The Chief Secretary to the Treasury (Peter Rees) was also the MP for Deal, which emerged as the favoured choice for a joint-services music school. However, the costs involved in doing so once again resulted in being more than the combined costs of the three schools staying put. Estimating that instead of saving £4m, the Deal scenario would actually cost £2.5m more. In February 1986 the Public Accounts Committee produced a report highly critical of the Government's economic argument. Lord Trefgarne, the Minister of State for Defence Support, informed the House of Lords of 'no prospect of Kneller Hall or the RAF school of music at Uxbridge being closed before 1989.'[85] The Royal Marines School of Music, meanwhile, moved to Portsmouth dockyard where it was initially housed at the former Royal Naval Detention Quarters with the cells converted to individual practice rooms.

In 1990 the Soviet Union collapsed and with it the Warsaw Pact. With a Soviet invasion of Western Europe no longer likely, a new government defence programme called Options for Change triggered the formation of the Corps of Army Music (CAMUS) where the number of army bands were reduced from 69 to 30. The Queen signed a warrant on 13 August 1994 to allow the formation of the newest and most junior Corps in the army. While the Household Cavalry and the Foot Guards retained their bands, many a proud regiment lost theirs in the transfer. CAMUS were established at Kneller Hall as the Headquarters of the Corps of Army Music and the Royal Military School of Music.

In the New Millennium CAMUS has progressed the traditional morale-boosting component in the use of contemporary music with even greater 'Oompah' with the Rhythm Force concerts the pinnacle, featuring Jools Holland as the special guest star in 2008 and 2009. In 2010 the Army rock bands performing at Kneller Hall were supported by Ray Quinn and Hayley Westenra. Status Quo played to a capacity crowd as part of a tour performing to troops on operations in Iraq, Afghanistan and The Falkland Islands. The Rhythm Force event became so popular that the Rugby Football Union in 2011 agreed to sponsor it as part of the Great River Race and Twickenham Riverside Regatta Weekend.

Rock & Pop gigs and Concerts in the Park at Kneller Hall continue to entertain the crowds on summer evenings, each performance showcasing talented musicians within Army Music. Entire families young and old haul-in picnics, cushions and chairs, unworried by soldiers wielding guns guarding the gates. Young, enthusiastic bandmasters variously introduce a rich variety of musical entertainment from pop bands to the long-established Last Night of the Proms concert. But the crowds are much reduced, as are the number of performances per season. And in an echo of David Shaw MP's criticisms regarding Deal, Kneller Hall has not been given the attention it should have been over the years

2016 – 2019

The Last Post?

When Defence Minister Mark Lancaster announced the release of 12 Ministry of Defence sites across the country as part of the department's drive for greater efficiency, he understood the feelings of the local community but insisted Kneller Hall was no longer fit for purpose. It was 'a stately home, not a school,' and to bring it up to standard for its current use would cost more than £30 million. 'Every pound we spend here is a pound that can't be spent on the front line,' he maintained, adding 'is spending that amount of money on a site which houses fewer than 75 staff really in the best interests of defence and military capability?' Chatham in Kent and Minley in Hampshire with the space and facilities to accommodate the Royal Military School of Music was the best use of public money.

It came as no surprise when local residents again stirred their Member of Parliament to convince government that a site of such key national, cultural and military heritage could not be sold off. A petition was signed by over 5,000 protestors condemning the proposed sale as an affront to the fabric of the borough. Lord True, the then Leader of Richmond-upon-Thames council, gave some consideration to the value of the estate from an historical and heritage perspective, as well as that of the Army. He recognised that rationalisation is often necessary and excess public assets should be sold. But Kneller Hall was of such importance not just to local, but national cultural and military heritage. 'It should not be tossed away to please junior accounting clerks at the Treasury with no understanding of the place in military history music in London's life and our nation's military history,' he concluded.[86]

The Better Defence Estate document published by the MOD in November 2016 has designated 2020 as the year of disposal for Kneller Hall.[87] An assigned architect has already drawn up plans for its development along with 20 other sites around the country. The Kneller Hall site looked to accommodate 192 new homes, a target easily achieved for Whitton with a minimum target for housing set at 150 units. Plans had already been drawn up by the MOD for 32 apartments created from the listed buildings and 117 flats, houses or duplexes outside of the Metropolitan Open Land. The cost to the MOD of retaining the Military School of Music was given as £30m to 'refurbish the ancient and inefficient Kneller Hall' and £14m to build single living accommodation. However, a Freedom of Information (FOI) request made by Twickenham's then Member of Parliament, Tania Mathias, revealed a total base estimate of £28.2m to demolish all the existing buildings and build new ones.[88] Refurbishing the Officers' public rooms would cost around £500,000 and band practice rooms a further £1.2m. It's not clear from this exchange precisely how much it would cost to bring the mansion itself up to scratch.

Following the long tradition of doing so, Sir Vince Cable, the current Member of Parliament for Twickenham, wrote to the Secretary of State for Defence, the Rt Hon Gavin Williamson MP in July 2018 about the proposed sale of Kneller Hall.[89] In his letter, Sir Vince considered the decision to close Kneller Hall as the home of the Military School of Music to be 'potentially an ill-judged, short-sighted decision.' As he understood it, the Hall was considered to be unfit for purpose and would cost in the region of £20m to bring the building up to standard. This, together with its listed status and metropolitan open land constraints made it an unattractive proposition to developers and potential buyers. The likelihood, as he saw it, was that the Army would be left with an empty building to maintain or forced to sell it off at a knock down price.

Sir Vince recalled 'a brilliant concert' he had attended at Kneller Hall where prominence was given to 'the fee-paying' Omani trainees. If the Hall were modernised, he suggested, then Kneller Hall could perform an important (and by implication lucrative) function training musicians from other countries such as Saudi Arabia and other Gulf States. 'It's not too difficult to see how a refurbished facility could be a money-spinning opportunity, as well as a generator of goodwill for the Army locally,' he closed. The notion of another Great British Centre of Excellence able to generate substantial income over time is an attractive proposition. The composer Howard Goodall observed

Ministers 'wouldn't dream of closing the Royal College of Music,'[90] which has a total income before donations and endowments of £17.9m per annum.

Further information privately obtained from the Ministry of Defence under the Freedom of Information Act indicates a relatively modest outlay per annum on the running of Kneller Hall. The average spend over the financial years 2006 and 2010 was £0.6m per annum; that between 2010 and 2015 had doubled to £1.2m per annum, and for the financial year 2015-2016 expenditure was estimated to be £1.1m.[91] At about an eighth of the price of a Challenger 2 tank, a world-renown centre of excellence for military band music could see a £30m public investment in Kneller Hall's cultural value extend far beyond what the real estate may be worth in financial terms.

In reply to Sir Vince's letter, The Right Honourable Tobias Ellwood MP, Parliamentary Under Secretary of State and Minister For Defence People and Veterans, underlined his responsibility of the Defence Estate in the MOD's commitment to provide effective support in defence capabilities and achieve the best value for money for the taxpayer.[92] He understood the strength of feeling with regard to Kneller Hall and the history and cultural significance the site holds within the local community but looked to the Joint Bands Project to consider the benefits of establishing a combined school of military music not at the 'ageing and inefficient' Kneller Hall. As to the sale of Kneller Hall itself, he added, 'the MOD are engaging with the local community and planning authority to decide the best future for the site, taking into account its listed building status.' At the point of publication that engagement is yet to take place.

Twenty months following the announcement of the sale of Kneller Hall, a Richmond Borough Local Plan Examination Hearing was held to respond to GVA, the company acting on behalf of the Ministry of Defence.[93] Modifications were required in order to be fully consistent with strategic planning in London involving a shared responsibility of the Mayor of London, the 32 London boroughs and the City of London Corporation. Under legislation establishing the Greater London Authority, the Mayor of London is required to produce and manage a spatial development strategy, or what is known as The London Plan. The annual target for Richmond borough from

2015 until the year 2025 was set at 315 dwellings per annum with Whitton deemed to have fallen short of the approximate number of units identified for it. The simple reason being there is no land left for development. The potential availability of the Kneller Hall estate therefore represented something of a windfall for all concerned.

In 2016 the Mayor of London published his new draft London Plan, raising Richmond-upon-Thames's 10-year target for net housing to over 8,000, or a 10% increase in housing across the borough incurring at least that much growth in population. The subsequent dent in the green aspirations of a local authority set against a housing target escalated by a revised London Plan need to be viewed against the realities of a 21st century Greater London. The vast majority of planned growth in Richmond borough had looked to come from small site development and residential street intensification across all wards. Whitton now looked more likely to bear the brunt in view of the proposed sale of the Kneller Hall. Lord True, as Leader of Richmond Council at the time of the MOD announcement observed, 'Whitton is rather more affordable than the rest of the borough….We don't want rich man's housing, thank you very much, we have enough already.'[94] Although the days of rich man's housing in Whitton have long since passed.

In looking back to look forward, the Army Music Museum archive at Kneller Hall holds an interesting box file containing a host of documents from the 1986 'rationalisation' of Kneller Hall either in the form of repair, sale, or tri-services propositions. One Defence Land Agent (London Region) document states that 'the planners in preparing their local plan did not take into consideration the possibility of a change of use for Kneller Hall except for the use of the under-used Twickenham Rugby Ground,' whatever that meant. The council back then looked upon the most favourable change of use of Kneller Hall as a hotel. A variety of prices were quoted across a choice of sale packages where the estimated value of the site including all the listed buildings and 14.24 acres of metropolitan open land complete with the sports pavilion and the Morris Hall came in at £3,338,000.

Although no date has been set regarding this latest rationalisation, the proposed Supplementary Planning Document (SPD) is looking to be adopted in its final form 'in the latter half of 2019'.[95] This is a process designed to build upon and provide more detailed guidance in the Local Plan that has again been prepared without taking into consideration possible changes of use for Kneller Hall. The SPD will consider consultation with developers, residents, businesses and local groups to form a strong, well-researched view to establish their priorities. A variety of views were expressed during the course of the 2018 Local Council Elections as to how the local community might benefit from a public open space in a part of the borough where such an amenity is rare. Suggestions include a swimming pool and / or ice rink, but even more modest provision such as that for dog-walkers and a variety of self-regulated sporting activities require access and maintenance in the form of costs to the council that would be issues.

The 'rationalisation' box file also holds the 1986 survey covering the repair and/or replacement of stonework, roofs, windows and other exterior decorations, the cost of which came in at £1,229,500. In their description of the estate for 'Richmond borough planning' published in June 1986, Chartered Surveyors Cluttons recognised the existence of a considerable number of fine mature trees but that 'this being government land the local authority was not empowered to make a tree preservation order.' Clearly times have changed with regard to the preservation provision that has been made for 300 trees in the grounds of the Kneller Hall estate that were granted protection as part of the previous local administration's expressed desire to retain the 12 acres of Metropolitan Open Land.

As to the estate's built history, the mansion itself bears only the name of the 17th century court painter to five monarchs with nothing of great historic interest attaching it before 1850. Historic England, the body tasked with protecting and preserving historic buildings provides a subdued listing of the mansion's external appearance in the form of it and the wall partially bounding the estate. Upon enquiry Historic England is not in a position to re-assess the estate to include the interior.[96] The office of local government responsible for safeguarding listed and other buildings of interest believes that the Guardhouse and the Band Practice Room are included but that's proved difficult to establish absolutely.

Above: Guardhouse.
Below: Band Room.

Things appear to have been more straightforward in 1986 when the Defence Land Agent (London Region) was able to confirm via a 'representative of the Listed Buildings Department of Richmond-upon-Thames council and a member of English Heritage' that the listed status extended to the Mansion, the Guardhouse, the Band Practice Room and the whole of the boundary wall including all the historic gates along Kneller Road to Whitton Dene, as far as Amberside Close.[97]

The interior of the mansion to the amateur eye consists of mostly unremarkable doorways and fireplaces across periods of later history. The run of reproduction Elgin marbles decorating the walls of the former dining room (now part of the museum) are of interest. These were a popular feature in educational establishments throughout the 19th century and is one of the few features dating from the failed teacher training college.

The chapel is another. It remains much as it was presented in 1848, except for the stained-glass window forming the central bay. This was enhanced by the military in 1909 to record the story of Kneller Hall from its beginnings as the mansion built for Sir Godfrey Kneller in 1709 to the founding of the School of Music by General H R H The Duke of Cambridge in 1857.

Other panels contain the names of serving Commandants, Directors of Music and Adjutants. The original panels are thought to have been plain, although there is no evidence for this. Claims that the 'magnificent oaken cupboards' and 'series of curious casts' remain 'as features from Sir Godfrey Kneller's tenure' are spurious.[98]

There is a similar structure to the current Guardroom shown on Kipp's drawing c1715 and again its footprint is included on the 1818 Enclosure Award map.

The building we see today is built of London stock with a slate roof and has all the attributes of 19th century architecture.

Interestingly, photographic evidence shows the front of the building to have been altered and the colonnade added, probably in 1923 when the former Students' Mess was converted into the Guardroom. The excellent condition of the clock tower also appears to chime with more recent times. Much of the open landscaping survives uniquely as one of three neighbouring gardens in the same district re-modelled according to the principles of Humphry Repton, the last great English landscape gardener.

In all of this it's easy to forget the focus is first and foremost a military establishment with a specific and important job to do.

Rudyard Kipling wrote in 1915:

> 'No one, not even the adjutant can say for certain where the soul of the battalion lives, but the expression of that soul is most often found in the band. A wise and sympathetic bandmaster can lift a battalion out of depression, cheer it up in sickness, and steady and recall it to itself in times of almost unendurable stress.'

But then it's easier to look back within the context of such words than it is to look forward as elected governments have done since 1934, each encountering the self-same difficulty in equating the value of retaining military bands against the necessary costs of equipment, personnel and weapons systems essential in the modern theatre of war.

Sources

Primary and Archival

London Borough of Richmond-upon-Thames Local Studies Collection

The Book of Twickenham.

The Twickenham Award 1818.

The New Assessment of the Parish of Twickenham, Middlesex, by Order of the Poor Law Commissioners for England and Wales. 22 June 1837.

Auction catalogue 29 July 1841: The Kneller Hall Estate, Whitton, Middlesex.

Borough of Twickenham Unitary District Council Minutes. Education Committee. 1. Trust Deeds. 2. Endowments of various schools. 27 May 1903.

Borough of Twickenham: Minutes of Proceedings. 1926–1965.

Borough of Twickenham: Notes on Invasion Defence. 1943.

London Borough of Richmond-upon-Thames Minutes of Proceedings 1965–1984.

London Borough of Hounslow Local Studies Collection:

Auction Catalogue: Kneller Hall Estate, Whitton, Dean, Twickenham.

National Archives

WO 78/2400/6. [Middlesex: Twickenham]. Plans and sections of buildings at the Royal Military School of Music, Kneller Hall. (married Quarters No.6 of batch).

WO 32/18307 Kneller Hall Middlesex: revision of boundaries and claim for right of way to stream.

WORK 6/184/7 Alterations, enlargement and furnishing, etc., following purchase by the Government. Subsequently transferred to the War Department 1847–1875.

ACC/1155 collection of architectural drawings (on paper) of Kneller Hall, Twickenham, by George Mair. 1848.

1910 Finance Act. Twickenham UDC.

London Metropolitan Archives

ACC/0780/075 Morris Emmanuel. Plan of freehold properties, including Kneller Hall, in Whitton (undated).

Kneller Hall Music of Army Music

Tanner, William C. (compiler and arranger) The Regular Army: Bandmasters' Who's Who. Unpublished.

Royal Military School of Music Historical Record (an indexed diary/scrapbook pertaining largely to the work of the school and events 1841–1978 rather than estate management).

Twickenham Museum

WW2 ARP diaries and local listings.

Welcome Library

http://archives.wellcomelibrary.org Reference SA/TIH/B/2/1/2: Civil Resettlement Units (CRU).

New York Botanical Garden

Humphry Repton *Red Book for Whitton*, Seat of Samuel Prime Esq. Reilley Collection 363. Reilley Coll in RBR. FDA690. W585 R4.

Parliamentary

https://api.parliament.uk/historic-hansard/lords/1854/feb/06/district-pauper-schools-question.

Parliamentary papers, Volume 21, Part 6, Minutes of Evidence from Rev. F. Temple, late Principal, Kneller Hall Training College. 27 January 1860.

Hansard 1803–2005. 13 May 1994; 21 November 1994. Commons Sittings. Remaining Private Members' Bills.

www.historyofparliamentonline.org The History of Parliament: British Political, Social and Local History.

www.gov.uk/government/organisations/defence-infrastructure-organisation Secretariat Defence Infrastructure Organisation 19 February 2016.

www.gov.uk/government/publications/better-defence-estate-strategy p19.

www.theyworkforyou.com/whall/?id=2016-02-24a.110.0 Westminster debates 24 February 2016.

www.richmond.gov.uk/media/14738/rep-059-001-defence-infrastructure-organisation-hearing-3-plus-4-statement.pdf.

www.publications.parliament.uk/pa/cm199394/cmhansrd/1994-05-13/Debate-12. House of Commons Hansard Debates: 13 May/21 November 1994.

www.historyofparliamentonline.org/volume/1820-1832/member/calvert-charles-1768-1832 The History of Parliament: British Political, Social and Local History. Member Biographies: Calvert, Charles (1768–1832) of Ockley Court, surr. and Kneller Hall, Whitton,

Newspapers and Periodicals

The Illustrated London News. 23 February 1850. p. 136.

The Graphic. Saturday 8 September 1894.

Gardening Magazine. (Vol.9. 1833). Extract.

The Times. 24 October 1970.

Richmond & Twickenham Times. 14 May 1972.

Richmond & Twickenham Times. 14 July 1972.

Richmond & Twickenham Times. 13 May 2002.

Richmond & Twickenham Times. 22 January 2016.

Hounslow Chronicle & Informer. 22 January 2016.

Richmond & Twickenham Times. 29 January 2016.

The Kneller Hall Trumpeter. Summer 2014 Issue 1.

Mail Online. 23 November 2018.

Maps

Moses Glover's *Survey of Isleworth Hundred*. 1635.

John Roque's *Survey of London and Environs*. 1741.

Plan of the Estate Situate at Whitton in the Parishes of Twickenham and Isleworth, Middlesex, for the sale by Messrs. Driver. 29 July 1841.

Plan of the Parish of Twickenham by W T Warren. 1846.

National Archives WO 32/18307 correspondence bundle with maps and sketches. Kneller Hall, Middlesex: revision of boundaries and claim for right of way to stream. OS Map. 1863.

Secondary Sources & Further Reading

Ironside, Edward. 1797. *The History and Antiquities of Twickenham.* London Borough of Richmond-upon-Thames Local Studies Collection.

Beavon, Charles. 1845. *Reports of Cases in Chancery: Argued and Determined in the Rolls.* Volume 6. Calvert v Godfrey. William Benning & Co. https://books.google.co.uk.

Buildings & monuments, modern and mediaeval (1850): www.islandguide.co.uk/middlesex/whitton.

The Spectator. http://archive.spectator.co.uk/article/11th-september-1909/10/netting-the-lake-at-kneller-hall.

Vaughan, H S. 1896. *The way about Middlesex (London).*

MacKenzie-Rogan, Lt.Col. John. 1926. *Fifty Years of Army Music.* Methuen & Co.

Stewart, Douglas J. 1971. S*ir Godfrey Kneller*. G. Bell & Sons.

Killanin, Lord. 1948. *Sir Godfrey Kneller and his times 1646–1723, being a review of English portraiture of the Period.* B.T. Batsford.

Urwin A C B. 1967. *Population and Housing in 1664.* Borough of Twickenham Local History Society.

Simpson, Donald. 1978. *The Twickenham of Laetitia Hawkins.* Paper No 39. Borough of Twickenham Local History Society.

Cashmore. T H R. 1977. *Twickenham in 1818: The Year of the Enclosure.* Borough of Twickenham Local History Society.

Cashmore T H R. 1980. *The Tithe Award: Twickenham in 1845.* Borough of Twickenham Local History Society Paper No 46.

Rosewarne. V.A. *A Brief History of Whitton* (unpublished). Local Studies Collection London Borough of Richmond-upon-Thames.

Rosewarne, V.A, *The Hearth Tax 1662–1689.* Twickenham Library transcription L336-22-TI. Local Studies Collection London Borough of Richmond-upon-Thames.

Rosewarne V.A. *Whitton Residents (1660–1714).* Local Studies Collection London Borough of Richmond-upon-Thames.

Pearce, Brian Louis. 1992. *The Fashioned Reed - the Poets of Twickenham from St Margarets to Hampton Court from 1500.* Borough of Twickenham Local History Society.

Foster. P and Simpson D H with revisions by Rosewarne, Vic. 1999. *Whitton Park and Whitton Place*. Borough of Twickenham Local History Society Paper No 41.

Barnfield, Paul. 2001. *When the Bombs Fell*. Paper No 80. Borough of Twickenham Local History Society.

Lockyer, Keira Quinn. 2010. *The Whitton legacy. The Story of Louis Kyezor. Kyezor, the King of Whitton*. Ballarat.

Harris. E. 2011. *Whitton Brook, Formerly Birket's Brook: A Small River Journey Through Whitton History*. The Borough of Twickenham Local History Society.

Harris. E. 2005. *Mr Giltrow's Enumeration: A Walk Through Whitton History*. Phantom Books.

Lockyer, Keira Quinn. 2017. *The Whitton Legacy: biography of Louis Kyezor 1794-1869*. Private publication.

David Englander, David. 1998. *Poverty and Poor Law Reform in Nineteenth Century Britain, 1834–1914*. Longman.

Williams, Karel. 1981. *From Pauperism to Poverty*. Routledge.

Dickens, Charles. 1850. *London Pauper Children: Household Words 1*, No23. pp. 459–552.

Newbold, David John. *British Planning and Preparations to Resist Invasion on LAND, September 1939–September 1940*. King's College, University of London. 1 August 2015 (including extracts from the diaries of Field Marshal Lord Ironside). https://kclpure.kcl.ac.uk/portal/.

Binns, Colonel P L. 1959. *A Hundred Years of Military Music: being the story of the Royal Military School of Military Music, Kneller Hall*. The Blackmore Press.

Turner, Gordon & Alwyn. 1996. *The Trumpets Will Sound: The Story of the Royal Military School of Music, Kneller Hall*. Parapress.

Fisher, D R. 2009. *The History of Parliament: The House of Commons 1820–1832*. Cambridge University Press.

Fitzgerald, Desmond. 1986. *A History of the Irish Guards in the Second World War*. The Irish Guards. pp199–203.

Warner, Philip. 1982. Phantom: *Uncovering the Secrets of the WW2 Special Forces Unit*. Pen & Sword.

McKinstry, Leo. 2014. *Sean Lion: The Failed Nazi Invasion that turned the tide of war*. John Murray.

Asher CJ Pirt. 2009. *2 GHQ Liaison Regiment Central Mediterranean. A record of its formation and History*. https://books.google.co.uk.

Historic Photographs and Illustrations

Whitton: The House of Sir Godfrey Kneller. Drawn and engraves by John Kip c1715. Plate 25 Alexander Pope's Twickenham. Borough of Twickenham Local History Society Occasional Paper No 3. 1988.

Sir Godfrey Kneller self-portrait c1720. Royal Military School of Music Museum Collection.

Sir Samuel Prime pen and ink sketch by George Townshend, 4th Viscount and 1st Marquess Townshend. National Portrait Gallery/Richard Cashmore Collection Twickenham Museum.

Humphry Repton engraving 1802 by W Holfeat after the Samuel Shelley Miniature. Private collection.

Whitton Hall watercolour by William Payne c1800. Ionides Collection. Orleans House Gallery, Twickenham.

Watercolour view south towards the rear of the house with the ornamental water painted either by Repton or William Payne from Repton's *Red Book for Whitton Hall*. New York Botanical Garden. Whitton, Seat of Samuel Prime Esq. Reilley Collection 363. FDA690. W585 R4.

Kneller Hall Training School. The Illustrated London News. 23 February 1850.

Ground Plan of Kneller Hall Training School. Royal School of Military Music Museum Archive.

English Heritage (NMR) RAF Photography. Sortie RAF/CPE/UK/2060. Frame 5185. 11 May 1947.

Endnotes

1. www.theyworkforyou.com/whall/?id=2016-02-24a.110.0.
2. Dr Farr, Statistical Superintendent, Registrar General's Department quote: *A Hundred Years of Military Music* p. 10.
3. Twickenham UDC *Minutes of Meetings: Health, Bathing and Allotments Committee.* January 1912.
4. Commanding Royal Engineers memo 7 July 1856 BB/4785 reproduced in *A Hundred Years of Military Music* p. 11.
5. A term found on deeds and other land documents north of the River Crane.
6. Hundred: A measurement of land consisting of 100 hides, a hide being one unit of land, which, like the acre, could vary depending on the soil and terrain. The earliest known basis of taxation in England, it continued after the Norman Conquest of 1066.
7. Hearth Tax 1662–1689 transcription. V A Rosewarne.
8. Sir Christopher Wren's name sometimes attaches its design without evidence. Sir John Vanbrugh is cited on the flyleaf of The Royal Military School of Music Historical Record flyleaf; again without any foundation.
9. Lord Killanin. Sir Godfrey Kneller and his times. p30. These paintings were left in his studio in Great Queen Street.
10. *The Twickenham of Laetitia Hawkins 1760–1835* pp. 14–16.
11. Owned by Edmund Hill the owner of the local gunpowder works.
12. A person employed on board a vessel by the owner of the cargo carried on the ship to manage and sell it and to buy goods for the return voyage.
13. *Whitton Park and Whitton Place* p. 45.
14. New York Botanical Garden. Whitton, Seat of Samuel Prime Esq. Repton Red Book Reilley Collection.
15. Reports of Cases in Chancery: Argued and Determined in the Rolls. Volume 6. Calvert v Godfrey. pp. 97–110.
16. *New Assessment of the Parish of Twickenham by order of the Poor Law commissioners for England and Wales*. 22 June 1837.
17. Kneller Hall Estate auction catalogue. 29 July 1841.

18. London Borough of Richmond-upon-Thames Local Studies Collection.
19. London Metropolitan Archives: Morris Emmanuel. Plan of freehold properties, including Kneller Hall, in Whitton (undated). ACC/0780/075.
20. *The Whitton legacy. The Story of Louis Kyezor. Kyezor, the King of Whitton.*
21. *Hansard: District Pauper Schools Question.* HL Deb 06 February 1854 vol 130 cc259–61.
22. Parliamentary papers, Volume 21, Part 6, Minutes of Evidence from Rev. F. Temple, late Principal. 27 January 1860.
23. *Buildings & monuments, modern and mediaeval* (1850).
24. National Archives: collection of architectural drawings (on paper) of Kneller Hall, Twickenham, by George Mair. 1848. ACC/1155.
25. *Buildings & monuments, modern and mediaeval* (1850).
26. Borough of Twickenham UDC Minutes. Education Committee. 1. Trust Deeds. 2. Endowments of various schools. 27 May 1903.
27. *A Hundred Years of Military Music* pp. 8–13.
28. National Archives: Alterations, enlargement and furnishing, etc., following purchase by the Government. Subsequently transferred to the War Department 1847-1875. WORK 6/184/7.
29. *A Hundred Years of Military Music.* p. 40.
30. *A Hundred Years of Military Music*: an account written in 1894 by a former student 1859–1861. pp. 59–61.
31. Adjutant General to Deputy Commissary General quoted in *A Hundred Years of Military Music* p. 44.
32. Reproduced extract in *A Hundred Years of Military Music* p. 110 gives 1882 as the year of publication, whereas the magazine was founded in September 1887.
33. 8 September 1894 pp. 273–4 erroneously citing neighbouring Whitton Park as the location.
34. Keyboard reed instrument invented by Victor Mustel (1815–90) of Paris. Of the harmonium type it contains some improvements to enhance dynamic expression.
35. As it was spelt prior to 1922 when changed to Whitton Dene.

36. National Archives: Kneller Hall, Middlesex: revision of boundaries and claim for right of way to stream. WO 32/18307 correspondence bundle with maps and sketches.

37. *The Graphic*. 8 September 1894 pp. 273–4.

38. Extracts from *Mr Giltrow's Enumeration: A Walk through Whitton History*.

39. National Archive – married quarters and boundary Kneller Hall: WO 78/2400/6. [Middlesex: Twickenham]. Plans and sections of buildings at the Royal Military School of Music, Kneller Hall. (no.6 of a batch).

40. *Way About Middlesex.* (1896) extract LBRuT Local Studies.

41. *The Spectator*. 11 September 1909 p. 10.

42. *A Hundred Years of Military Music.* p. 70.

43. Henry Stanhope. *The Times*. 24 October 1970: Army Bands Under Fire.

44. *RMSM Historical Record*. 1914.

45. Kneller Hall Museum Archive.

46. Kneller Hall Museum Archive.

47. *Fifty Years of Army Music*.

48. *RMSM Historical Record.* p. 50.

49. Courtesy Nick Bentley.

50. *The Regular Army: Bandmasters Who's Who*, compiled and arranged by William C Tanner. Kneller Hall Museum Archive lists Burkmann and Ramsey but not Rowbotham. The War Graves Commission and London Borough of Richmond-upon-Thames Cemeteries list Burkmann as Burkmarr.

51. *Richmond & Twickenham Times*. 13 May 2002.

52. Paul Barnfield, *Borough of Twickenham Local History Society Newsletter*, September 2018.

53. The reference to which a group of musical instruments are tuned for a performance.

54. Auction Catalogue: Kneller Hall Estate, Whitton, Dean, Twickenham.

55. Borough of Twickenham Minutes of Proceedings. General Matters 30 May 1933.

56. Borough of Twickenham Minutes of Proceedings. General Matters. 10 June 1933.
57. Borough of Twickenham Minutes of Proceedings: Kneller Hall Removal. 13 April 1934.
58. Borough of Twickenham Minutes of Proceedings: Town Planning Scheme / War Department Land 4 July 1933; Kneller Hall Removal 7 April 1934; Letter from Country Treasurer 27 April 1934; General Matters 16 May 1934; Town Planning: War Office Property 4 November 1935; War Office Lands 9 April 1936; Town Planning: Kneller Hall Grounds 14 May 1936; Town Planning 20 June 1936.
59. London Borough of Richmond-upon-Thames Local Studies Collection.
60. Newbold, David Anthony (undated King's College dissertation) British planning and preparations to resist invasion on land, September 1939 - September 1940. https://kclpure.kcl.ac.uk/portal/. p. 22.
61. Diaries of Field Marshal Lord Ironside, 27 May 1940 Newbold, David Anthony (undated King's College dissertation) British planning and preparations to resist invasion on land, September 1939 - September 1940. P. 136.
62. *Operation Sea Lion*. pp. 38–39.
63. British planning and preparations to resist invasion on land, September 1939 - September 1940. p. 248. The school has since moved to Barnes.
64. 2 GHQ Liaison Regiment Central Mediterranean. A record of its formation and History. p. 9.
65. London Borough of Richmond-upon-Thames Local Studies Collection.
66. Barnfield, Paul. 2001. *When the Bombs Fell: Twickenham, Teddington and The Hamptons under Aerial Bombardment during the Second World War*. Borough of Twickenham Local History Society Paper No 80.
67. Twickenham Museum.
68. Fitzgerald, Desmond. 1986. *A History of the Irish Guards in the Second World War*. The Irish Guards. pp. 199–203.
69. http://archives.wellcomelibrary.org Reference SA/TIH/B/2/1/2: Civil Resettlement Units (CRU).
70. Borough of Twickenham: Minutes of Proceedings. 11 May 1945; Health & Allotments. 14 July 1945.

71. Borough of Twickenham: Minutes of Proceedings. Expected Applications. 3 June 1949.
72. Borough of Twickenham: Minutes of Proceedings. 4 August 1949; 2 December 1949.
73. Borough of Twickenham: Minutes of Proceedings. 3 February 1950.
74. A corruption of 'Cut-Through Alley' from the days when student bandsmen looked to avoid being put on a charge for returning late to barracks. Subsequently named Spray Lane.
75. Borough of Twickenham: Minutes of Proceedings. 3 March 1950; 31 March 1950.
76. Bob Wood, landlord of the Duke of Cambridge who studied at Kneller Hall with the South Wales Borderers. His brother Brian was a student in 1962 when he was part of the band for the scene.
77. Royal School of Military Music Museum Archive.
78. *The Times*. 24 October 1970.
79. Quoted in *The Trumpets Will Sound.* p. 12.
80. *Richmond & Twickenham Times*. 14 May 1972.
81. *Richmond & Twickenham Times*. 14 July 1972.
82. The concerts reverted to Wednesdays in 1984.
83. *The Trumpets Will Sound.* p. 120.
84. House of Commons Hansard Debates: 13 May / 21 November 1994. publications.parliament.uk/pa/cm199394/cmhansrd/1994-05-13/Debate-12.html.
85. *The Trumpets Will Sound.* p. 125.
86. *Richmond & Twickenham Times*. 29 January 2016.
87. www.gov.uk/government/publications/better-defence-estate-strategy p.19.
88. www.theyworkforyou.com/whall/?id=2016-02-24a.110.0 Westminster debates 24 February 2016.
89. 20 July 2018 circulated to Dr Cable MP's Twickenham constituents.
90. *Mail Online*. 23 November 2018.
91. Secretariat Defence Infrastructure Organisation. 19 February 2016.
92. Received by Sir Vince Cable MP. 15 August 2018.

93. September 2017 www.richmond.gov.uk/media/14738/rep-059-001-defence-infrastructure-organisation-hearing-3-plus-4-statement.pdf .

94. *Richmond & Twickenham Times*. 29 January 2016.

95. Email: Cabinet Member for Environment, Planning and Sustainability, LB Richmond-upon-Thames. 5 July 2018.

96. Email correspondence between urban-design@richmond.gov.uk and Historic England April–May 2018.

97. OS map attaching the 1986 tri-services proposition highlights these features.

98. *The Graphic*. Saturday 8 September 1894.

ACKNOWLEDGEMENTS

MANY THANKS AS ever for all the help and assistance generously supplied by Jane Baxter and staff of London Borough of Richmond-upon-Thames Local Studies Collection. Thanks too to Nick Bentley, military historian; Stephen Sinon, Curator of Special Collections, Research and Archives, New York Botanical Garden; Mertz Library; Sir Vince Cable MP; Councillor Martin Elengorn, Cabinet Member for Environment, Planning and Sustainability, London Borough of Richmond upon Thames; Nicolette Duckham, Senior Conservation Officer Environment Directorate, Richmond and Wandsworth Councils; Patience Trevor, Historic England; and Esther Mann, Curator, Museum of Army Music, Kneller Hall. Thanks also to the Publications Committee, Borough of Twickenham Local History Society, whose painstaking efforts to proof this publication is to be admired as much as it is appreciated. And to Alan Roe and Rosemary McGlashon for making it all technically possible in this electronic age. Finally, thank you to all the students and pupils at Kneller Hall whose practice and performances have added to the joy of living close to this proud institution.

ALSO BY ED HARRIS

Whitton Brook: Formerly Birket's Brook
A Small River Journey Through Whitton History

This rare union of Twickenham and Isleworth local history will be of interest to those living both sides of the Richmond-upon-Thames and Hounslow borough divide. It makes for a fascinating story of a modest stream that has served for centuries as the parish and borough boundary, and which survives, in part, despite the indifference of both local authorities and the predations of big business. Its 68 pages are complemented with 50 photos, illustrations and maps in black and white and colour; some never before published. Included is a full-colour pull-out reproduction of Moses Adams' 1842 survey of Twickenham copyhold land held in Isleworth parish showing the course of the brook from the site of Whitton Park to Moor Mead with all the modern day landmarks indicated.

To order this book, please visit www.botlhs.co.uk

Borough of Twickenham Local History Society

The Society was formed in 1962 to promote interest in, and record the history of, Twickenham, Teddington, Whitton and the Hamptons. We meet for illustrated talks on the first Monday of the month from October to May in St Mary's Church Hall, Church Street, Twickenham at 8pm. Our newsletter is published three times a year with numerous articles of local historical interest and we have visits to places of interest locally and further afield. The Society is a prolific publisher of historical research papers with over 100 titles many of which are still in print.

Recent titles include:

- **"The Hidden Area of Teddington": The Growth of Fulwell 1870-1939** *(Paper 102)* by Dr Christopher French £6.00
- **Radnor House, Twickenham: The Story of a Thames-side House** *(Paper 101)* by Mike Cherry £5.00
- **"The Italian Murder" and the Slums of Victorian and Edwardian Kingston** *(Occasional Paper 10)* by Dr Christopher French £4.00
- **Images of Hampton in the 1920s and 1930s** *(Paper 100)* by John Sheaf £7.50
- **"A Life Well Led": Richard Gardner (1842-1918) and the City and Metropolitan Police Orphanage, Twickenham** *(Paper 99)* by Dr Christopher French £6.00
- **The Fallen of St Mary's Parish, Twickenham 1914-1918** *(Paper 98)* by Jeremy and Sue Hamilton-Miller £8.00
- **Down The Drain: Local Public Sewage Developments 1863-1899** *(Paper 97)* by Ray Elmitt £10.00
- **A Suburb of Contrasts: Udney Park Estate, Teddington 1870-1939** *(Paper 96)* by Dr Christopher French £5.50
- **Hampton 100 Years Ago** *(Paper 95)* by John Sheaf £6.00
- **"I have a weak heart and military service would knock me up"** *(Paper 94)* by Paul Barnfield £5.50

For details of all our publications please visit our website at www.botlhs.co.uk.
Membership information is available from:

Borough of Twickenham Local History Society
Membership Secretary
87 Fifth Cross Road
Twickenham, TW2 5LJ